THE UNDERTAKING

Philip Osment

THE UNDERTAKING

OBERON BOOKS

LONDON

First published in 1997 by Oberon Books Ltd (incorporating Absolute Classics)
521 Caledonian Road, London, N7 9RH
Tel: 0171 607 3637 / Fax: 0171 607 3629

ISBN 1 870259 87 4

Cover design: Andrzej Klimowski

Typography: Richard Doust

Printed by Rexam Digital Imaging Limited, Reading

PREFACE

The Undertaking was commissioned by Gay Sweatshop and was written in 1995 in consultation with James Neale Kennerley the director.

In writing the play I wanted to look at the lives of people who had been involved with the politics of the 70s. Now they are living in different times: AIDS has inevitably altered their attitudes towards their sexuality and the current political climate has forced them to reassess their ideals.

I was particularly interested in their relationships with their families. The generation that benefitted from the post war education policies and the Welfare State were often educated out of their class and lost contact with their roots. For Gay people, leaving their families and home towns to seek a more tolerant cosmopolitan milieu, was sometimes a matter of life and death. But this amputation of the past can create people who feel maimed and incomplete. In working on the play we discovered that all of the characters are looking for a sense of completion. For Michael, as a Gay Irish man living in London, this feeling of imcompleteness is particularly acute.

My other consideration in writing the play was to show people on a journey. I was interested in the tensions and personal crises that this can engender – and the comedy that ensues. This was my final concern: to write a comedy (with echoes of *A Midsummer Night's Dream*) in spite of the serious nature of the journey. I wanted to show people who lose control of events – and themselves – the further they get from London; who are bewitched, bothered and bewildered the deeper they get into the Irish countryside; but who leave this enchanted domain wiser and made whole.

I would like to thank Willie Elliott, Pete Freer, Joanne O'Brien and most particularly Lin Coghlan, Nina Ward and James Neale Kennerley for their help and advice.

Philip Osment
London 1997

Characters

MICHAEL
SHEILA
EAMON
HOWARD
PATRICK

THE UNDERTAKING was first performed at Leicester Haymarket Studio on February 21st 1996, produced by Gay Sweatshop Theatre Company, with the following cast:

MICHAEL, Liam Halligan

SHEILA, Patricia Ede

EAMON, John Lloyd-Stephenson

HOWARD, Derek Howard

PATRICK, Gary Lilburn

DIRECTION: James Neale-Kennerley

DESIGN: Annabel Lee

SCENE ONE

The back garden of SHEILA's house in London. One exit leads to the house and the other to where the van is parked. Bags that have been packed are lying around ready to be put in the van. MICHAEL is surrounded by his tent untangling the guy ropes. SHEILA enters with a cup of coffee and surveys her garden.

SHEILA: You asked John next door to water the flowers while we're away?

MICHAEL: Mmmm.

SHEILA gets out her mobile phone and dials.

MICHAEL: Hope all the poles are here.

SHEILA: Hello, could I speak to the Style Section please. Picture editor.

MICHAEL: Where's the mallet?

SHEILA: Hello. Hi, Mehmet it's Sheila Marks. Look, when do you need those photos? Tomorrow? No, it's just that I'm going to Ireland today.

MICHAEL: Sheila!

SHEILA: (*Points.*) Will you send your bike? Oh, alright, seeing as it's you.

MICHAEL: Where?

SHEILA: (*Points again.*) Yeah, we're nearly packed. Just the three of us – me and Michael. And Howard. He was the lover of Henry who died.

MICHAEL: I can't see it.

SHEILA: (*Picking up the mallet and giving it to him.*) To be honest a trip to Ireland's the last thing I need. I'm so busy. Mmmm. Well, anyway I'd better phone my bike. OK. Bye.

She dials again.

MICHAEL: I'm sure some of the poles are missing.

SHEILA: (*Dialling.*) Honestly! He didn't tell me he needed those photos today. (*Into the phone.*) Hello, it's Sheila Marks, can you send a bike over please. To go to the Sunday Times. OK, thanks.

MICHAEL: I thought you weren't going to work for the Murdoch press.

SHEILA: (*Fatalistic.*) I know.

MICHAEL: You used this last you know.

SHEILA: I didn't.

MICHAEL: You did. You went to Greenham on that shoot.

SHEILA: That was years ago.

MICHAEL: It's the last time it was used.

SHEILA: Were there any more poles in the cupboard?

MICHAEL: No.

SHEILA: Let's see.

MICHAEL: It's my tent for God's sake!

SHEILA: Hold that.

MICHAEL: Sheila, there's no point.

SHEILA: Now....

She starts to assemble the poles.

MICHAEL: Why've you given me this?

SHEILA: Don't want to get it mixed up with those other bits.

MICHAEL: Jesus!

SHEILA: What's wrong?

MICHAEL: Drives me crazy when you do that.

SHEILA: What?

MICHAEL: Give me things and expect me to hold them for you.

SHEILA: What are you talking about?

MICHAEL: You did it in Sainsburys yesterday.

SHEILA: What?

MICHAEL: Gave me your purse to hold while you fished in your bag.

SHEILA: You still going on about that?

MICHAEL: You could've put it in your pocket but you wanted me to stand there holding it for you.

SHEILA: For God's sake. You make such a fuss.

MICHAEL: I'm trying to do this. (*Looking at what she's doing.*) That doesn't go like that.

SHEILA: Have you set the timer on the video? That Bergman film's on tomorrow night.

MICHAEL: Which one?

SHEILA: *Wild Strawberries.*

MICHAEL: Is that the one on the island?

SHEILA: No. It's the one where the professor goes back to his home town.

MICHAEL: Oh, I like that one.

SHEILA: Remember we saw it together at the Ritzy?

MICHAEL: 1979.

SHEILA: What's this for?

MICHAEL: To put under the pole. Stop it making a hole in the ground-sheet.

SHEILA: You sure you didn't use it last?

MICHAEL: Last time I used it was when Henry and I went to Cornwall.

SHEILA: When was that?

MICHAEL: 1982.

SHEILA: When did I go to Greenham?

MICHAEL: 1983.

SHEILA: You sure?

MICHAEL: Yes.

SHEILA: Don't know how you can remember that.

MICHAEL: Henry had just bought his house. You were going to help us move in but you couldn't because you were at Greenham. We moved into the house in May eighty-three. QED.

SHEILA: God you've always got to be right, haven't you?

MICHAEL: I am always right.

They laugh.

MICHAEL: (*Struggling with the guy strings.*)Damn. Bloody mad idea.

SHEILA: What?

MICHAEL: The whole thing. We should just fly to Dublin. Costs a fortune to go on the ferry. Plus we have to get to Holyhead.

SHEILA: We wouldn't be able to take all the camping stuff on the plane.

MICHAEL: No. We could stay in Bed and Breakfast.

SHEILA: And seeing as we've got Henry's van now.

MICHAEL: You know how much it rains in Ireland?

SHEILA: Anyway I thought you said this island won't have any hotels on it.

MICHAEL: No, it's uninhabited now. I suppose when Henry used to go there as a kid people still lived there.

SHEILA: So we'll have to camp.

MICHAEL: When I was young we went camping every summer. Had to share a tent with my brother. Lough Derg, Donegal, Connemara. Always rained.

SHEILA: This is how Howard wants to do it.

MICHAEL: Oh well, if Howard wants to do it like this, then this is how we'll have to do it. After all she's the grieving widow.

SHEILA: Michael.

MICHAEL: What?

SHEILA: I hate it when you do that.

Pause. She has given up on the tent and is loading a film into her camera.

SHEILA: It was Henry's idea anyway.

MICHAEL: (*Looking up.*) I hope you're appreciating all this, Henry. Still calling the tune, aren't you?

SHEILA: I'm only taking one body.

MICHAEL: Eh?

She holds up the camera.

MICHAEL: Oh. Howard wants it all faithfully documented.

SHEILA: We're supposed to do it at sunset, aren't we?

MICHAEL: Think so.

SHEILA: Means I'll have to take a flash.

MICHAEL: God! Howard will probably put on antlers and expect us to prance round him in the nude.

SHEILA giggles.

MICHAEL: You know he went off to Norfolk last week.

SHEILA: Yeah. To celebrate the summer solstice.

MICHAEL: With a coven.

SHEILA: No!

MICHAEL: He thinks he's a bloody white witch.

SHEILA laughs again.

MICHAEL: To think he used to be a computer programmer.

She laughs.

SHEILA: Hope he doesn't find it all too much.

MICHAEL: Hope I don't find Howard too much.

SHEILA: It's just a few days out of your life. Least you're on holiday. I've got all this work I should be doing.

MICHAEL: Mmm.

SHEILA: And you probably need to do something like this.

MICHAEL: Why?

SHEILA: To say goodbye to Henry.

Pause.

MICHAEL: Will you look at this mark on my leg?

SHEILA: Michael!

MICHAEL: I don't know what it is.

SHEILA: It won't be anything.

MICHAEL: It's like a bruise.

SHEILA: For God's sake, Michael. You had the test. It was negative.

MICHAEL: Mmmm.

SHEILA: Let's see.

MICHAEL: No, it's alright.

SHEILA: Come on.

MICHAEL: No, you're right.

SHEILA: Let me see.

He rolls up his trouser leg.

SHEILA: Where is it?

MICHAEL: There.

SHEILA: Where?

MICHAEL: There.

SHEILA: What there?

MICHAEL: No there.

SHEILA: What that?

MICHAEL: Yes.

SHEILA: Can hardly see it.

MICHAEL: What is it though?

SHEILA: Have you banged your leg lately?

MICHAEL: No.

SHEILA: What about last night? You walked into the coffee table.

MICHAEL: Oh yes.

SHEILA: It was that leg, wasn't it?

MICHAEL: I forgot.

She laughs.

MICHAEL: I didn't know what it was.

SHEILA: You're such a hypochondriac.

MICHAEL: Don't know what's wrong with me at the moment.

SHEILA: Well, it's understandable. It's scary.

MICHAEL: Always get like this when I'm anxious.

SHEILA: What are you anxious about?

MICHAEL: Work.

SHEILA: Mmm.

MICHAEL: I just don't know whether to go back in the autumn. More and more students, fewer and fewer staff. They want me to teach structuralism next term on top of everything else. I feel like I'm drowning.

SHEILA: Are they going to pay you more?

MICHAEL: Are they heck!

SHEILA: The students would miss you.

MICHAEL: Doubt it.

SHEILA: They all think you're wonderful. You're their Daddy.

MICHAEL sighs.

SHEILA: What would you do?

MICHAEL: I don't know.

SHEILA: Write?

MICHAEL: Huh!

SHEILA: You're always saying you want to.

MICHAEL: Yeah, well....

SHEILA: And you could afford it now with the money Henry's left you.

MICHAEL: As executor you're not supposed to discuss the will with any of the benificiaries.

SHEILA: Crap! I could sell this place and we could buy somewhere together in the country.

MICHAEL: Mmmm.

SHEILA: You ought to get that tent packed.

MICHAEL: What's the point if we haven't got all the poles?

SHEILA: We could all sleep in the van.

MICHAEL: It isn't big enough.

SHEILA: There are three bunks.

MICHAEL: Yeah, but there's four of us.

SHEILA: Eh?

MICHAEL: And we won't be taking the van onto the island anyway.

SHEILA: Four?

MICHAEL: Yes.

SHEILA: Who's the fourth?

MICHAEL: Eamon.

SHEILA: Eamon?

MICHAEL: Yes.

Pause.

MICHAEL: I told you.

SHEILA: When?

MICHAEL: Last week.

SHEILA: You said he'd mentioned something.

MICHAEL: Yes.

SHEILA: But then you didn't say anything else about it.

MICHAEL: Well, he decided to come.

SHEILA starts to go.

MICHAEL: Where are you going?

SHEILA: Have a look in the cupboard under the stairs for these poles.

MICHAEL: For Jesus sake, Sheila.

SHEILA: What?

MICHAEL: He got very close to Henry.

SHEILA: Yeah well, he's attracted to the tragedy of it all. He's like a groupie.

MICHAEL: He's a nurse.

SHEILA: Why didn't you tell me he was coming?

MICHAEL: I did.

SHEILA: You didn't.

MICHAEL: Did.

SHEILA: Look....

MICHAEL: What?

SHEILA: Is that who you're having a relationship with?

MICHAEL: What do you mean?

SHEILA: Well you have been stopping out a lot lately.

MICHAEL: We've slept together.

SHEILA throws her hands up in exasperation.

MICHAEL: What?

SHEILA: Why can't you just tell me things?

MICHAEL: I thought you knew.

SHEILA: So since when?

MICHAEL: I don't know.

SHEILA: Michael.

MICHAEL: A week or so.

SHEILA: Right.

MICHAEL: For God's sake we're not married.

SHEILA looks at him.

MICHAEL: I don't have to ask your permission, do I?

SHEILA: You could have just told me instead of making me guess.

MICHAEL: Oh fuck off! I won't go on the bloody trip.

SHEILA: Fuck off yourself.

The doorbell rings.

SHEILA: Hope that's the bike.

She goes. MICHAEL kicks the tent-poles. EAMON enters.

MICHAEL: Hello.

EAMON: Hi.

They kiss.

MICHAEL: Mmmm, it's nice to see you.

EAMON: (*Playacting schoolboy.*) Oh, Mr Donnelly, sir, you haven't shaved.

MICHAEL: Sorry.

EAMON: No, I like it.

They kiss.

EAMON: You ought to grow a goatee.

MICHAEL: You think?

EAMON: It would suit you man.

MICHAEL: Give me more gravitas would it?

EAMON: Eh?

MICHAEL: Make me look older and wiser.

EAMON: Gravitas. You packed that book you were going to lend me?

MICHAEL: Which one?

EAMON: The one you were talking about last night after the film.

MICHAEL: The Foucault? Yeah.

EAMON: Wish you'd been my teacher at Tulse Hill Boys.

MICHAEL laughs. They kiss.

EAMON: You get much writing done last night?

MICHAEL: Bit.

EAMON: You should have brought me back. I'd've got your juices flowing.

MICHAEL: Would you?

EAMON: You never bring me back here.

MICHAEL: I like staying at yours.

EAMON: Be great to spend a whole week together.

MICHAEL: Yes. I'm really looking forward to it. Showing you Ireland.

EAMON: You know what you were saying the other night?

MICHAEL: What?

EAMON: About maybe moving to Galway.

MICHAEL: Oh. Yes.

EAMON: Well I was thinking I'd like to find out about Health Education over there.

MICHAEL: Right.

EAMON: See if there's any job possibilities for me.

MICHAEL: (*Uncertainly.*) Mmmm.

EAMON: What?

MICHAEL: Nothing. Come here.

EAMON: You're so masterful.

> *They are kissing as SHEILA enters with more tent-poles. MICHAEL defiantly keeps his arm around EAMON.*

MICHAEL: Where were they?

SHEILA: In that banner you made.

MICHAEL: What banner?

SHEILA: Clause twenty-eight.

MICHAEL: Ohhhhhh.

> *She starts to pack up the poles.*

EAMON: He tell you about the film we saw last night, Sheila?

SHEILA: No. Where did you go?

EAMON: The Screen.

MICHAEL: Where's the bag?

SHEILA: In the kitchen.

EAMON: I'll get it.

EAMON goes. SHEILA is struggling with the poles.

MICHAEL: Here.

SHEILA: I can manage.

Pause.

SHEILA: Good film, was it?

MICHAEL: OK.

SHEILA: I thought we were going to go and see it when we came back from Ireland.

MICHAEL: There wasn't anything else on I fancied.

Pause.

MICHAEL: Look, I'm sorry. I should have told you.

SHEILA: It was supposed to be just the three of us. Henry's closest friends.

MICHAEL: So you don't like Eamon.

SHEILA: He's not someone I'd necessarily choose to go away with. I'm sure he's really sweet. But he's not exactly an intellectual giant, is he?

EAMON returns.

EAMON: (*Handing SHEILA the bag.*) Here you are.

SHEILA: Thanks.

EAMON: You wanna joint, Sheila?

SHEILA: Um, OK.

MICHAEL: We'll have to be going soon.

SHEILA: Howard's not here yet.

EAMON: He's going to be late.

MICHAEL: How come?

EAMON: He was seeing an aromatherapy client at ten. Then he had to go to the hospital. Here's one I prepared earlier.

He hands the joint to SHEILA.

MICHAEL: Have you spoken to him then?

EAMON: I called in on him on my way home last night.

MICHAEL: (*A bit miffed.*) Oh.

SHEILA: How was he?

EAMON: Bit shaky. He's being very together though.

SHEILA/MICHAEL: Mmmm.

EAMON: I like Howard.

SHEILA: Is this grass?

EAMON: Yeah.

SHEILA: It's great.

EAMON: I've got some of those tablets you asked me about at the funeral as well.

SHEILA: What some – ?

EAMON: Yeah.

SHEILA: What do I owe you?

EAMON: It's OK.

SHEILA: Don't be daft.

She gets out her purse.

MICHAEL: Are you two going to spend the whole week on drugs?

SHEILA: (*Giving EAMON the money.*) Here.

EAMON: No way.

MICHAEL: What's wrong with Howard anyway?

EAMON: He's not sleeping.

MICHAEL: Bad conscience.

SHEILA: Michael.

MICHAEL: What?

EAMON: What you mean?

MICHAEL: All the rows he had with Henry over the past couple of years.

SHEILA: It was hard for both of them.

EAMON: I think he's getting night sweats.

SHEILA: Anyway you and Henry used to row.

EAMON: Don't you like Howard?

MICHAEL: It's not that.

SHEILA: Isn't it?

MICHAEL: Howard's always found it difficult that I've known Henry so much longer than him. I mean, we met in Dublin during my first year at Trinity for God's sake! And that was...well...a long time ago.

SHEILA: Nineteen seventy-one?

MICHAEL: Seventy two.

EAMON: I was five in nineteen seventy-two.

SHEILA laughs.

SHEILA: Honestly, the rows they used to have! Remember my birthday party that time?

MICHAEL: Give us a hand, Eamon.

EAMON: What happened?

SHEILA: Michael gave Henry a black eye.

EAMON: No!

SHEILA: He did.

EAMON: Why?

MICHAEL: Can't remember. Here.

EAMON and MICHAEL start to fold the tent.

SHEILA: Henry was kissing this boy I knew from the I.M.G.

EAMON: What's the I.M.G.?

MICHAEL: International Marxist Group. She was a member.

EAMON: Were you a terrorist?

SHEILA: No. It was a left wing party.

MICHAEL: She used to stand outside Highbury Corner tube selling the paper every Saturday.

SHEILA: Yeah we thought politics could change things then. Or some of us did.

MICHAEL: Meaning I didn't?

SHEILA: No!

MICHAEL: Her lot used to think that Gay politics were a diversion from the class struggle.

SHEILA: That was the W.R.P.

MICHAEL: All those arguments.

SHEILA: Those were the days.

EAMON: So what happened at this birthday party?

SHEILA: So when Michael saw Henry kissing this boy he poured the washing-up bowl over his head.

EAMON: (*Laughing.*) Wicked!

MICHAEL: (*About the tent.*) Right that's that done.

SHEILA: I was running about trying to move my stereo out of their way.

EAMON laughs more.

MICHAEL: Wasn't that the night you ended up rolling about the floor in tears because of that bloke from Trops Out?

SHEILA: Then Michael chased Henry out into the street and Henry jumped into a cab. So Michael got in too. Then Henry jumped out the other side and Michael followed him. The poor taxi driver didn't know what was happening.

EAMON: Sounds like a film.

MICHAEL: She spent the whole night sobbing because of this bloke. "Why do relationships do this to me?"

SHEILA: So then they ran back inside and Michael punched Henry and Henry fell down the stairs.

EAMON laughs.

MICHAEL: No he didn't.

SHEILA: Yes he did.

MICHAEL: He fell down the stairs later because he was pissed.

SHEILA: He didn't.

MICHAEL: He did.

EAMON: All sounds a bit wild.

MICHAEL looks at his watch.

MICHAEL: I'll put this in the van.

He takes the tent to the van.

SHEILA: (*Calling after him.*) Don't forget you have to set the timer on the video.

She grimaces.

EAMON: What?

SHEILA: He doesn't like me getting stoned.

EAMON: He smokes dope.

SHEILA: Very rarely.

EAMON: He likes it in bed.

SHEILA: Oh well....

EAMON: It's great for sex, dope.

SHEILA: Mmmm.

Pause.

EAMON: I'm glad you and me are going to get to know each other better.

SHEILA: Yes.

EAMON: How long have you and Michael lived together?

SHEILA: Well, we all three squatted together in the late seventies. Then they moved into Henry's house. When I bought this place Michael and Henry were splitting up so Michael moved in with me. Ten years.

EAMON: How did you get to know them anyway?

SHEILA: I met Henry at Troops Out.

EAMON: What's Troops Out?

SHEILA: God, Eamon!

EAMON: What?

SHEILA: Troops out of Northern Ireland!

EAMON: Was Henry involved with the IRA?

SHEILA: No! He's Protestant anyway. Was Protestant.

EAMON: But he was from Dublin.

SHEILA: Yeah but his ancestors came from England. Anglo-Irish, see?

EAMON: Oh.

SHEILA: That was another of their favourite disputes. Who was most Irish.

The doorbell goes.

MICHAEL: (*Entering from the van.*) I'll go.

SHEILA: The photos are on the hall table if it's the bike.

He crosses to the house.

EAMON: You're good mates aren't you, you and Mike?

SHEILA: Mmmm.

EAMON: It's nice you've got each other.

SHEILA: Yes.

EAMON: You know, you're good friends. But it's not sort of complicated by sex and stuff.

SHEILA: No.

HOWARD and MICHAEL enter. HOWARD has all his bags.

SHEILA: Howard! There you are.

HOWARD: Sorry I'm late.

SHEILA: You've got a lot of bags.

HOWARD: It's my costume that takes up the room.

SHEILA: Your costume?

HOWARD: For the ceremony.

EAMON: You should see it. He showed it me last night. Looks great.

MICHAEL: Where's my map?

SHEILA: What map?

MICHAEL: The road map.

HOWARD: I've bought Henry's one of Ireland.

MICHAEL: We need one of England and Wales.

SHEILA: I haven't had it.

MICHAEL: You borrowed it to go to Scotland on that shoot.

SHEILA: I didn't.

MICHAEL: You did.

HOWARD: Can I wash this celery?

MICHAEL: We can stop and eat on the motorway.

HOWARD: I can't eat motorway food, Michael.

SHEILA: Help yourself.

He goes. MICHAEL makes a face at his back. SHEILA signals to him to stop. EAMON looks from one to the other.

SHEILA: Do you think that's it?

MICHAEL: Probably.

EAMON: What?

SHEILA is approaching the bag.

MICHAEL: Sheila, don't.

SHEILA: I can't see. It could be.

EAMON: What do you think it is?

MICHAEL: The urn.

EAMON: What?

MICHAEL: The ashes.

EAMON: Oh.

SHEILA: It is. Look.

MICHAEL: Sheila!

She takes it out. Suddenly HENRY is present. They all look at the urn lost in their thoughts.

MICHAEL: He's coming.

SHEILA hurriedly puts the urn back in the bag and runs back to EAMON.

SHEILA: Where is he?

MICHAEL: He's gone back in.

SHEILA suddenly sees the funny side and starts giggling – partly at the fright she got and partly because of the solemnity of the previous moment. EAMON laughs too.

MICHAEL: You're stoned.

EAMON and SHEILA are helpless with laughter.

MICHAEL: Honestly! Shhh!

HOWARD returns. He has a plate of celery, a carrot, some water biscuits and a glass of orange juice. He takes out a little bottle and drips brown liquid into the orange juice.

HOWARD: Have you had the van checked out, Michael?

MICHAEL: I got the mechanic down the road to service it.

HOWARD: Henry always goes to the Volkswagen dealer in St. John's Wood.

MICHAEL: He's really good, this bloke.

HOWARD: Mmm.

SHEILA: What's that Howard?

HOWARD: Echinacea. It strengthens the immune system.

Pause.

SHEILA: I'll see if I can find this map.

She goes.

EAMON: How was it at the hospital?

HOWARD: They say my blood count's quite high.

EAMON: You see Dr. Ford?

HOWARD: Yes.

EAMON: She's good.

HOWARD: Apparently Peter's dying.

MICHAEL: Oh dear.

HOWARD: Yes. And Steve's not very well either.

EAMON: Peter who I met?

MICHAEL: No.

HOWARD: We'll have a few more funerals to go to when we get back.

MICHAEL: You don't know.

HOWARD: It's one of the few things you can depend on, Michael. For some of us it's part of our lives now.

EAMON: Yeah.

Pause. Everyone nods and looks thoughtful. SHEILA returns.

SHEILA: Is this it?

MICHAEL: Where was it?

SHEILA: In your bookcase.

MICHAEL: Oh.

EAMON: Are we going on the M1?

MICHAEL: M40. Then the M6.

HOWARD: It's better to go on the M42 and the M5.

MICHAEL: M5?

HOWARD: You miss out Spaghetti Junction.

MICHAEL: It's not the way I'd go.

HOWARD: It's the way Henry always went to Snowdonia.

MICHAEL: M40, M42, M6, M54.

HOWARD: No. M40, M42 going the other way, M5.

SHEILA: Can everyone play?

MICHAEL: The other way?

HOWARD: Yes. Underneath Birmingham.

SHEILA: (*In a posh voice.*) Em thirty-nine. How old are you?

MICHAEL: What do you mean underneath Birmingham?

EAMON: Em twenty-eight.

SHEILA: So young!

HOWARD: Here, I'll show you.

HOWARD tries to get hold of the map.

MICHAEL: Hang on.

He pulls the map away.

SHEILA: Oh God, boys and maps!

EAMON giggles.

MICHAEL: There, look.

HOWARD: Yes, but it's much better to go underneath Birmingham like that.

MICHAEL: Looks further.

HOWARD: But it's quicker.

MICHAEL: Why?

HOWARD: Because you always get traffic jams around Spaghetti Junction.

SHEILA: He's right. We got really held up there going to Glasgow.

MICHAEL: Well, I'd rather go the way I know.

SHEILA: What's the difference?

HOWARD: You see, Eamon. Which way looks quicker to you?

EAMON: (*Looking at the map.*) This way?

HOWARD: (*Triumphantly.*) Exactly!

MICHAEL: We ought to be going.

SHEILA: I'm waiting for this bike.

HOWARD is now looking at the map of Ireland he's brought.

HOWARD: When we get to Dublin it looks fairly straight-forward.

MICHAEL: I don't need a map to get from Dublin to Kerry.

HOWARD: I'll navigate. Henry always said I was a good navigator.

MICHAEL: (*Picking up Howard's bag.*) I'll put this in the van.

EAMON: Want some help?

MICHAEL: OK.

He goes. EAMON picks up the bag with the urn.

HOWARD: I'll take that.

EAMON puts it back and goes with the other bags.

HOWARD: Dublin, Kildare, Limerick, Tralee. All these lakes.

SHEILA: Michael was brought up near Limerick. On a farm.

HOWARD: Really?

SHEILA: His brother still lives there.

HOWARD: We'll be able to call in on him.

SHEILA: I don't think so.

HOWARD: Why not?

SHEILA: Michael doesn't get on with him. When we went to Dublin together he didn't even tell them he was over there.

HOWARD: Has he got lots of brothers and sisters?

SHEILA: No. There was a sister. She died quite young.

HOWARD: Oh.

SHEILA: There was a big fuss about him being gay. So it'd be awkward seeing Eamon's with us.

HOWARD: I didn't even know Eamon was coming till last night.

SHEILA: Really?

HOWARD: I thought it was just going to be the people Henry was closest to.

SHEILA: Eamon got to know Henry quite well.

HOWARD: Still. I mean I like Eamon but Michael shouldn't have assumed it was OK for him to just tag along. Weren't you pissed off?

SHEILA: It's what people do when they're in a new relationship.

HOWARD: I thought the whole thing was so insensitive.

SHEILA: What?

HOWARD: Henry lying there dying and Michael getting off with his nurse.

SHEILA: It wasn't quite like that.

HOWARD: Henry knew it was going on.

SHEILA: They didn't get together until last week.

HOWARD: Eh?

SHEILA: What?

HOWARD: It's been going on for weeks. They had sex in the broom cupboard at the hospital once.

SHEILA: At the hospital?

HOWARD: Yeah.

SHEILA: Eamon could have got the sack.

HOWARD: The night of the funeral they came back here and screwed. You'd taken Henry's sister back to Chatham. I didn't feel like going back to the house so Michael gave me his room. Woke up in the middle of the night, heard them banging away next door.

SHEILA: In my room?

HOWARD: Must've been. Making a terrible racket. Not very tactful.

MICHAEL enters.

MICHAEL: The van's packed.

SHEILA: Right.

Doorbell rings.

SHEILA: That'll be that bike.

She goes.

MICHAEL: You ready?

HOWARD: Nearly.

HOWARD munches his celery. MICHAEL watches.

SCENE 2

A quiet country roadside. SHEILA and HOWARD are sitting under a big umbrella.

HOWARD: I'm so tired.

SHEILA: Did you get any sleep on the boat?

HOWARD: No.

SHEILA: Me neither.

HOWARD: If we'd caught the afternoon boat we'd have been able to stay overnight in Dublin in a nice B and B.

SHEILA: Mmmm.

HOWARD: If we hadn't got stuck at Spaghetti Junction we wouldn't have missed it.

SHEILA: No.

HOWARD: We should have gone on the M5.

SHEILA: Yes.

HOWARD: I told him.

SHEILA: I know.

Pause.

SHEILA: They've been gone ages.

HOWARD: Maybe that house doesn't have a phone.

SHEILA: Can't understand why my mobile doesn't work over here.

HOWARD: He should have taken the van to a proper Volkswagen dealer before we left.

SHEILA: He's actually very good that mechanic.

HOWARD: Henry drove all over the country and we never broke down once.

SHEILA: Well, don't go on about it to Michael, Howard.

HOWARD: I know he's touchy, isn't he? He wouldn't even let me navigate. We wouldn't have broken down in the middle of nowhere if he'd listened to me.

SHEILA: Well, he wanted to show us Lough Derg.

HOWARD: We haven't seen it though, have we? This is practically a farm track. Leading to a peat bog. I told him it would be a dead end.

SHEILA: There weren't any signposts.

HOWARD: They obviously don't believe in them in Ireland.

SHEILA: I guess the roads have all changed since he lived here.

HOWARD: The way he jumped down your throat when you asked him if he knew where we were.

SHEILA: He's tired.

HOWARD: Don't know why you let him get away with it. He's worse than my Dad with my Mum.

Pause.

SHEILA: Maybe he'll phone his brother.

HOWARD: How near does he live?

SHEILA: Can't be far.

HOWARD: Do you think he will?

SHEILA: Don't know.

HOWARD: He could at least tow us to a garage.

SHEILA: Yes.

HOWARD: Don't you get fed up with it?

SHEILA: What?

HOWARD: Michael and his moods.

SHEILA: Most of the time we get on really well.

HOWARD: It isn't as if....

SHEILA: What?

HOWARD: Well, he's gay.

SHEILA: I know.

HOWARD: I mean it's not as if it's a sexual relationship.

SHEILA: Mind.

HOWARD: What?

SHEILA: Your leg's getting wet.

HOWARD moves his leg.

HOWARD: Don't you miss sex?

SHEILA: How do you know I'm not having it all the time?

HOWARD: Are you?

SHEILA: Of course.

She laughs.

HOWARD: I slept with someone in Norfolk last week.

SHEILA: That's good.

HOWARD: Mmmm.

SHEILA: No?

HOWARD: Bit of a disaster.

SHEILA: Oh dear.

HOWARD: I only did it to see what it would feel like.

SHEILA: Maybe it was too soon.

HOWARD: He was an acupuncturist from Thetford.

SHEILA: Right.

HOWARD: When was the last time for you?

SHEILA: Oh, I don't know.

HOWARD: It's really important that all that energy doesn't get blocked inside you. There's this really good aromatherapy treatment for freeing your libido.

SHEILA: Oh, Howard!

SHEILA: What?

SHEILA: You're falling for the myth.

HOWARD: What you mean?

SHEILA: That everyone's having sex all the time. Most people aren't.

Pause.

HOWARD: Henry said you really wanted a child.

SHEILA: Did he?

HOWARD: Yeah.

SHEILA: I don't know if I'd make a very good parent.

HOWARD: Course you would.

SHEILA: When would I have time anyway? With my work!

HOWARD: Mmmm.

SHEILA: Anyway I wouldn't want to bring up a child on my own.

HOWARD: That's why you split up with Steve, isn't it?

SHEILA: What?

HOWARD: Cause he didn't want children.

SHEILA: We weren't very compatible.

HOWARD: I liked him. He was sexy.

SHEILA: He was a flirt. It's not quite the same thing. Where are they?

HOWARD: What happened to that bloke in Henry's chambers?

SHEILA: Lionel?

HOWARD: That's him.

SHEILA: Oh dear!

HOWARD: What?

SHEILA: I'm not that desperate, Howard.

HOWARD: I thought he was OK.

SHEILA: Would you go out with him?

HOWARD: He's not gay is he?

SHEILA: If he was.

HOWARD: That's hypothetical.

SHEILA: He was really seedy.

HOWARD: Henry thought your relationship with Michael was stopping you getting involved with anyone else.

SHEILA: I don't want a relationship with Lionel! For God's sake, Howard! I'm perfectly happy as I am. Everyone thinks that if you're not having sex then you're not living. Maybe I don't want that distraction in my life. It takes up so much time and energy for a start. Sex is the big panacea of our age. People think it will give their lives a meaning if they can only find that special person to have sex with. Makes me sick!

Pause.

HOWARD: Here they are.

SHEILA: About time.

HOWARD: (*Calls.*) Any luck?

MICHAEL: (*Off.*) The garage doesn't have a breakdown service.

HOWARD: What?

MICHAEL and EAMON enter.

MICHAEL: They don't have a pick up truck.

HOWARD: For God's sake! What sort of a garage is that?

SHEILA: Did you look up Volkswagen dealers?

MICHAEL: The farmer said he'd give us a tow when his son gets back with their land-rover.

EAMON: But that might not be till late.

HOWARD: Why didn't you just phone the Volkswagen dealer?

MICHAEL: Because there isn't one near here.

HOWARD: There must be.

MICHAEL: There isn't.

HOWARD: So we're stuck here all day.

MICHAEL: I'm sorry. It's not my fault.

EAMON: You should have seen the way that woman was staring at me.

HOWARD: Probably never seen anyone Black before.

MICHAEL: Don't be stupid.

EAMON: Made me feel really uncomfortable.

SHEILA: Good job she didn't know you're gay as well.

HOWARD: She probably doesn't know what a homosexual is.

MICHAEL: Ah, to be sure, they round your sort up and put them in the jail, Howard. And then they burn you alive after mass on the Sabbath. Then they parade around the village with your head on a pole. Sure tis a terrible backward place an all an all.

Silence. The others grimace at each other.

SHEILA: Do you think it would be any use phoning your brother?

MICHAEL: What for?

SHEILA: See if he can come and rescue us.

EAMON: I suggested that.

HOWARD: How far away does he live?

MICHAEL doesn't answer. EAMON shrugs at HOWARD.

SHEILA: Michael?

MICHAEL: What?

SHEILA: Would it be far for him to come?

MICHAEL: Not really.

SHEILA: So, why don't you phone him?

MICHAEL doesn't answer.

EAMON: I could do with a drink.

SHEILA: We could get out the camping stove.

MICHAEL: They probably won't be there.

SHEILA: Why not?

MICHAEL: They'll be out working. Farmers don't tend to
have mobile phones.

HOWARD: Wouldn't do them much good. Sheila's didn't
work here.

SHEILA: You could try.

Pause.

SHEILA: Couldn't you?

MICHAEL: That woman's going to be fed up with us.

EAMON: She won't mind.

SHEILA: Do you want me to come with you?

MICHAEL: It's up to you.

SHEILA: Come on then.

MICHAEL: Why don't we just wait for this land-rover?

SHEILA: Could be late before he gets here.

HOWARD: The garage could be shut by then. And it's
Sunday tomorrow.

MICHAEL: Oh, you're the expert on the opening times of Irish garages, are you, Howard?

SHEILA: Michael!

MICHAEL: I thought maybe you'd have fixed the van by the time we got back seeing as you know everything.

SHEILA: Come on.

MICHAEL and SHEILA go.

EAMON: It's stopped raining.

HOWARD: For the moment.

EAMON: Yeah.

HOWARD: Hope the weather's not like this on the island. Henry said sometimes they had to wait for days to get across if the weather was bad.

EAMON: Did they live there?

HOWARD: No they lived in Dublin but they had a holiday cottage there.

EAMON: You ever go there with him?

HOWARD: No. He was going to bring me. We ran out of time. We went to Galway once.

EAMON: What's it like?

HOWARD: We had a great time.

EAMON: Does it have a gay scene?

HOWARD: It didn't then.

EAMON: I'd like to go there.

HOWARD: We could go back that way.

EAMON: Henry never thought of moving back then?

HOWARD: No way.

EAMON: Mike was talking about getting a house over here the other night.

HOWARD: Really?

EAMON: Yes.

HOWARD: I suppose he could afford it now.

EAMON: Yeah?

HOWARD: Henry's left him all that money.

EAMON: Has he?

HOWARD: Hasn't he told you?

EAMON: No.

HOWARD: Yes.

EAMON: He was a really kind bloke.

HOWARD: Sheila helped him draw up the will. But I think Henry was a bit confused. You know how he was at the end. I don't think he'd have wanted me to move out and sell the house.

EAMON: No?

HOWARD: He always said I could live there as long as I wanted. But now with the will like that, it has to be sold so that the capital can be shared between me and Michael.

EAMON: I see.

HOWARD: It's hard to leave somewhere we've shared for so long. It's all I've got left of him.

EAMON: You won't have to do it right away will you?

HOWARD: I've already had a letter about it from the solicitors.

EAMON: Mike wouldn't want to rush you out.

HOWARD: I assume he knows all about it. Or maybe
Sheila's behind that too.

EAMON: Yeah?

HOWARD: You know how close they are. They're like a
married couple really.

EAMON: Mmmm.

HOWARD: Still there's nothing I can do about it now.
Henry's signature is on the will. I'm not about to
contest it.

EAMON: No.

HOWARD: We hardly saw anything of Michael all last year.
Henry asked him to come round to help sort out all his
papers from the seventies. You know how they used to
publish that magazine together – *Leftward Gays* whatever
it was called.

EAMON: Yeah?

HOWARD: Took Michael six months to do anything about
it. Time he did, Henry was too ill to tackle it. So all his
personal papers never got sorted out.

EAMON: Shame.

HOWARD: You know what he said the day Henry died?

EAMON: No.

HOWARD: Said it was a relief.

EAMON: I spose he meant he wasn't suffering no more.

HOWARD: People can be so fucking selfish.

He starts crying.

EAMON: Hey man.

HOWARD sobs. SHEILA enters. EAMON looks at her meaningfully. SHEILA ignores him. She goes and puts her arm around HOWARD.

SHEILA: It's OK, Howard. Here.

She gives him a tissue.

SHEILA: Sorry it's a bit shredded but it's clean.

HOWARD and SHEILA laugh.

SHEILA: Howard I'm sorry I snapped.

HOWARD: It's OK.

SHEILA: Everyone's a bit strung out.

HOWARD: Mmmm.

SHEILA: He's probably up there saying, "Look at them, God, they can't do anything right without me."

HOWARD: Yeah.

SHEILA: You want a cup of tea?

HOWARD: Tea and sympathy.

SHEILA: That's right.

HOWARD: Did he get through?

SHEILA: Think so. He didn't want me listening in.

She picks up a water container.

HOWARD: (*To EAMON.*) Sorry about that.

EAMON: It's OK.

He puts his arm around HOWARD. MICHAEL enters.

EAMON: Is he coming?

MICHAEL: Yeah.

EAMON: Will it take long?

MICHAEL: Shouldn't think so.

SHEILA: I was going to make a drink.

MICHAEL: There's some lager in the van.

SHEILA: I'll try and get that stove of Henry's to work.

HOWARD: I'll do it. There's a knack.

SHEILA: I'll go down and fill this up then.

HOWARD: Make sure there aren't any dead sheep in that
stream.

SHEILA: Ugh.

HOWARD goes.

EAMON: Poor Howard.

MICHAEL: What?

EAMON: He's a bit upset.

MICHAEL: Playing for sympathy, was he?

SHEILA: Michael, stop it.

MICHAEL: Oh, I'm the villain now, am I?

MICHAEL goes.

EAMON: He needed to cry.

SHEILA: Mmmm.

EAMON: It's good for him.

SHEILA: Just don't get off on it too much Eamon.

EAMON: What?

SHEILA: Other people's grief.

*She goes. EAMON is gobsmacked. MICHAEL returns with some
cans of lager.*

MICHAEL: Bloody Howard with that stove. Drive you mad!

EAMON: Mmmm.

MICHAEL: You want one?

EAMON: No thanks.

MICHAEL opens a can.

EAMON: So what's he like, your brother?

MICHAEL: He's a farmer. He's married with two kids. And he's thick as pig shite.

EAMON: Is he as sexy as you?

MICHAEL: Don't know.

EAMON snuggles up to MICHAEL. MICHAEL forces himself to smile. EAMON whispers in his ear.

MICHAEL: Well you turn me on too.

EAMON puts his hand inside MICHAEL's shirt.

MICHAEL: (*Nearly spilling his lager.*) Mind.

EAMON pinches his nipple.

MICHAEL: (*Annoyed.*) Aowwhh.

EAMON: Sorry.

MICHAEL: It's OK.

EAMON kisses him. SHEILA enters.

MICHAEL: Got the water?

SHEILA: Is that a bull?

MICHAEL: Which one?

SHEILA: That one.

EAMON: Looks a bit fierce.

MICHAEL: Don't be daft.

She goes to boil the water.

EAMON: Fancy a little walk?

MICHAEL: Where to?

EAMON: Thought we might find a nice quiet spot to have a lie down.

MICHAEL: The grass will be wet.

EAMON: Under a bush.

MICHAEL doesn't move.

EAMON: So did Henry leave you his house?

MICHAEL: Who told you that?

EAMON: Howard.

MICHAEL: What's he been saying?

EAMON: Nothing.

MICHAEL: He left it to both of us. Did he say he'd left it just to me?

EAMON: No.

MICHAEL: So what was he saying?

EAMON: I think he's worried about having to move out.

MICHAEL: Is he saying I'm making him move out?

EAMON: No.

MICHAEL: He's got his own flat you know. And we're not making him move till he's ready.

EAMON: Shhh.

HOWARD returns.

HOWARD: Won't be long now.

He sits with them.

HOWARD: So how does it feel to be back, Michael?

MICHAEL: It never changes.

HOWARD: You really thinking of moving back here?

MICHAEL: Get fed up with London sometimes.

HOWARD: What would you do?

EAMON: He's been offered a job.

HOWARD: Oh yes? Where?

MICHAEL: Galway.

HOWARD: (*He now understands EAMON's interest in Galway.*) Ahhhh!

MICHAEL: It's only part time.

HOWARD: You could spend the rest of the time writing.

MICHAEL: Maybe.

HOWARD: Isn't that what you've always wanted to do?

MICHAEL: Don't know.

EAMON: You should have a go.

HOWARD: Yes.

EAMON: Howard says we could go to Galway on the way back.

MICHAEL: It's a bit out of the way.

HOWARD: Lot of English yuppies are moving to Ireland. They say it's a better world to bring their children up in.

MICHAEL: Mmmm.

HOWARD: Henry never wanted to come back.

MICHAEL: I know.

HOWARD: It's so backward. Be hell being gay here.

MICHAEL: It's got a lower age of consent than England.

HOWARD: Couldn't live with all that Catholicism. See those nuns on the boat?

He crosses himself.

HOWARD: Gives me the creeps.

MICHAEL: Why?

HOWARD: Look at the way the Catholic Church has oppressed women and gay men over the centuries.

EAMON: Always thought that most priests were gay. That's why they become priests isn't it?

MICHAEL: What are you talking about?

EAMON: So they can wear frocks.

SHEILA enters with a tray of mugs. HOWARD makes a great show of not being sexist.

HOWARD: Look at us leaving you to make the tea.

EAMON: You want some help?

SHEILA: The water's boiling.

EAMON goes to get the water.

HOWARD: Were your parents orthodox, Sheila?

SHEILA: Eh?

HOWARD: We were talking about religion.

SHEILA: My grandparents were.

HOWARD: So you didn't have to go to Synagogue.

SHEILA: No. I sometimes wondered what I missed out on.

HOWARD: No!

SHEILA: I know. I never thought I'd say that either. We all used to think we didn't need religion. But now... I don't know... maybe it's just about getting older.

EAMON returns with the water.

SHEILA: Give it here.

HOWARD: Let me do it.

EAMON: I'll do it.

SHEILA looks on wryly.

SHEILA: I suppose we all have a need for ritual.

HOWARD: Yeah but traditional religious rituals have lost their meaning.

MICHAEL: So you think we should be going out in the woods and taking our clothes off instead?

HOWARD: The older religions have got a lot to teach us. More and more people are getting interested in them.

MICHAEL: I know, I've seen all the stalls at Pride. All those New Age therapies. Acupuncture, massage, gay Buddhists.

HOWARD: It's very good that as gay people we're looking for new ways of expressing our spirituality.

MICHAEL: I can remember when it was called Gay Pride and it was about a political movement. Now G.L.F. gets a slot on the main stage in between the Smirnoff ads and the soap stars. The whole event has been hijacked by consumerism for God's sake.

HOWARD: What's that got to do with spirituality?

MICHAEL: The interest in New Age philosophies is just another manifestation of the rejection of political action in favour of individual solutions.

SHEILA: You can tell he's a teacher!

HOWARD: Well I don't agree with you Michael.

MICHAEL: I didn't think that you would.

HOWARD: People are just trying to understand their place in the cosmos. It's because they're suddenly being confronted with death.

EAMON: Sugar, Howard?

HOWARD: No thanks.

EAMON hands the tea round.

SHEILA: Funny to think our whole world is made up from a dead star.

EAMON: What you mean?

SHEILA: You don't know your Joni Mitchell. That's what we're made of.

MICHAEL: Jesus!

SHEILA: What?

MICHAEL: I can't believe I'm listening to this crap. I'm afraid you won't get me to join in with any shamanistic ritual with the ashes, Howard. You won't be persuading me that they're really star-dust.

HOWARD: You'd rather go to mass, would you? Maybe you should take that job and move back here.

SHEILA: What job?

MICHAEL: Been offered a bit of lecturing.

EAMON: In Galway, Sheila. You ever been there?

SHEILA: No.

MICHAEL: I haven't decided anything.

EAMON sits down beside Michael.

EAMON: (*To HOWARD.*) Do you think there are jobs in health awareness over here?

HOWARD: Probably.

EAMON touches MICHAEL on the back of the neck. Because of the tension he is feeling he starts and knocks tea all over EAMON.

EAMON: Aowhh.

MICHAEL: I'm sorry.

SHEILA: I'll get a cloth.

She goes.

HOWARD: Let's see.

EAMON: It's OK.

HOWARD: Let me mop you up.

He uses SHEILA's tissue.

EAMON: Thanks. Mmmm.

HOWARD: What?

EAMON: Feels nice.

HOWARD: (*Laughing.*) What that?

EAMON: Bit lower.

HOWARD tickles EAMON. EAMON retaliates. They laugh.
SHEILA returns.

SHEILA: Alright?

EAMON: Yeah. Get off Howard!

EAMON starts tickling HOWARD. HOWARD laughs. SHEILA
looks at MICHAEL.

SCENE 3

The same. Later that day. HOWARD and EAMON.

HOWARD: What time is it?

EAMON: Half eight.

Sound of cow mooing. EAMON looks at it warily.

EAMON: Is that the bull?

HOWARD: I don't know.

EAMON: Don't like the look of him, innit?

HOWARD: I think it's a cow.

SHEILA enters.

EAMON: OK?

SHEILA: Patrick wants a cup of tea.

EAMON: The water's just boiled.

He pours water into a mug. Cows moo.

SHEILA: Go away!

HOWARD: Any luck?

SHEILA: No. They keep talking about the transmission and
the fuel pump and the distributor cap.

HOWARD: Hope we're not going to be stuck here all night.

SHEILA: Mmmm.

HOWARD: Why can't he just tow us to a garage?

SHEILA: He said it will be shut by now.

HOWARD: I said that.

SHEILA: I know.

EAMON: (*Calling.*) Your tea's here.

HOWARD: He's attractive, isn't he?

SHEILA: You think so?

HOWARD: Definitely. They don't seem very close, do they?

SHEILA: They're not.

HOWARD: The way they greeted each other!

EAMON: "Hello, Michael." "Patrick." "How you been?" "Fine." "Yourself?" "Grand."

HOWARD laughs. SHEILA is still being frosty with EAMON because of the revelation about Galway.

SHEILA: They haven't seen each other for years.

HOWARD: Michael's pretending to be all butch as well.

They all laugh. MICHAEL and PATRICK enter.

MICHAEL: Glad someone's laughing.

SHEILA: Is it working?

MICHAEL: No.

PATRICK: We'll give it another go in a minute.

MICHAEL: I don't think it's going to start.

PATRICK: I've cleaned the plugs. Michael didn't know how to clean the plugs. Can you believe that? You'd flooded the engine with all your attempting to get it started. Once you've flooded the engine you've to wait.

MICHAEL: I know that.

PATRICK: He was never the practical one. Remember the time you were trying to mend the puncture on your bike and the dog ran away with the inner tube, Michael?

MICHAEL: Yes.

PATRICK: We looked out the window and there was Michael running around the field after the dog. Every time he stopped the dog would stop and turn around and laugh at him.

SHEILA laughs.

PATRICK: Michael was swearing his head off. The air was blue around him.

SHEILA: (*Laughing.*) He gets very ratty when he's mending things anyway.

PATRICK: You're right there, Sheila.

SHEILA: I always keep out of his way when he's doing DIY around the house.

PATRICK: You've not changed then, Michael.

SHEILA: Doesn't sound like it.

PATRICK: You can imagine the sort of things he was saying to the dog then, Sheila. He ended up throwing the bicycle wheel at her. The dog ran off with the inner tube still in her mouth and half the spokes on the wheel were broken.

EAMON, HOWARD and SHEILA all laugh at MICHAEL.

PATRICK: Dad was furious, so he was. It was a brand new bike, Sheila.

SHEILA: Really?

MICHAEL: It was second hand. We never got anything new.

EAMON: (*Handing PATRICK his tea.*) Here.

PATRICK: Thank you.

Cows moo. EAMON is frightened and moves away from them.

PATRICK: I'll tell you something, Michael, you could do with getting a new van if you ask me.

MICHAEL: What's wrong with it?

PATRICK: Why do you want to go driving Sheila around in an old heap like that? I'd've thought a college lecturer would be able to buy himself a proper car.

MICHAEL: It'll be great for holidays.

PATRICK: I always hire a car when we go on holiday. We went to Marbella last year, you know, Michael?

MICHAEL: Really?

PATRICK: Norah had always wanted to go to Spain. We got a grand car at Malaga airport.

MICHAEL: Actually the van belonged to Henry.

PATRICK: Oh well...

SHEILA: Did you like Spain?

PATRICK: It was OK. Do you know Marbella, Sheila?

SHEILA: I've driven through.

PATRICK: It's a grand place.

MICHAEL: If you like that sort of thing.

PATRICK: What?

SHEILA: Lot of English.

PATRICK: Ah, well, you can't have everything.

HOWARD, EAMON and SHEILA laugh.

PATRICK: To be honest it wasn't the English that bothered me. It was the way those African fellas pestered you on the beach. You couldn't get a moment's rest without them coming up and asking you to be buying their rubbish. "Nice wallet. Very nice. Good wallet. You want look? But you get the likes of them everywhere I suppose.

MICHAEL: What do you mean?

PATRICK: Eh?

MICHAEL: The likes of them?

PATRICK: You know what I mean.

MICHAEL: Black people.

PATRICK: Don't you be starting, Michael, and you only just over.

HOWARD: What do you think is wrong with the van?

PATRICK: What do you mean by saying a thing like that? They were forever pestering you. Would you like that? Would he like that, Sheila?

SHEILA: He got very cross with people hassling us in Egypt last Christmas.

PATRICK: Are you saying I'm racist? He's calling me a racist, Eamon. I'm not a racist.

SHEILA: Michael thought it was something to do with the petrol supply.

PATRICK: We get black people over here now, Michael? Did you not watch Ireland in the World Cup? There's a fella I know in Limerick. He's a Negro. He's a grand fella, Eamon. You'd like him.

EAMON: Yeah?

PATRICK: How did you get an Irish name anyway?

EAMON: My Mum's mother was Irish.

PATRICK: You're codding me.

MICHAEL: Lots of Irish women in London marry Black men.

PATRICK: Is that a fact?

SHEILA: So do you think it is the petrol supply, Patrick?

PATRICK: You might be needing a new fuel pump.

HOWARD: Oh dear.

PATRICK: Barney's garage won't have one of those. He'd have to get one from Limerick. I'll tell you something that Linford Christie is a wonderful runner. Do you know him, Eamon?

MICHAEL: Just because he's Black, it doesn't necessarily follow that Eamon is personally acquainted with him.

PATRICK: That's not what I meant. You're twisting my words Michael.

EAMON: I know who he is.

PATRICK: And who's the one that runs the hurdles for England?

MICHAEL: Eamon doesn't like sport.

EAMON: Colin Jackson.

PATRICK: No, not that one. He's retired now, the one I'm thinking about.

HOWARD: Chris Akubussi.

PATRICK: That's the one. I always liked him.

MICHAEL: Grand fella. Always laughing.

PATRICK: What?

SHEILA: So how long do you think it will take?

PATRICK: What's this now?

HOWARD: To get the fuel pump from Limerick.

PATRICK: Well, it's Sunday tomorrow.

HOWARD: I know.

PATRICK: I brought a rope with me. I'll tow you back to the farm if I have to.

MICHAEL: If you took us to the garage we could camp there overnight. Maybe he'd look at it in the morning anyway.

PATRICK: On a Sunday! He'll be after charging you a fortune.

MICHAEL: Can't be helped.

PATRICK: You'd be mad to be camping. Sure the sky will come down on your heads.

HOWARD: Looks as if it's going to start raining again.

PATRICK: It does sure enough. You'd better all come to the farm.

MICHAEL: We'll be alright.

PATRICK: It's no trouble at all. You used to hate camping. I don't know why you didn't ask if you could stay with me in the first place. Can you believe that? Me own brother comes all the way to Ireland and doesn't even tell me he's here.

MICHAEL: We were going to go straight to Dingle.

PATRICK: What do you think of that, Sheila?

SHEILA: I don't know.

MICHAEL: I didn't think you'd have room.

PATRICK: Norah's away with the kids.

MICHAEL: Oh right.

PATRICK: So there's no problem with beds. We can put these two fellas in the boys' room. I'll sleep in the attic. And you and Sheila can have our bed.

SHEILA: It's very kind of you.

MICHAEL: Bit far to tow, isn't it?

PATRICK: Sure we'll be there in no time at all.

MICHAEL: Well, it might start anyway.

Cow moos. EAMON jumps. SHEILA and HOWARD are also very wary.

SHEILA: Is that a bull, Patrick?

PATRICK: It might be.

EAMON and SHEILA react.

MICHAEL: For God's sake!

EAMON: Me and my boyfriend got lost once because we were scared of walking through a field of bulls.

HOWARD: Nelly queens!

MICHAEL: How long will it take us?

PATRICK: An hour.

HOWARD: I got chased by a bull once.

EAMON: Where was that? In the back room at the L.A.?

HOWARD: Ha ha. It was on this farm where Henry and I stayed.

EAMON: Hope you didn't have your high heels on at the time.

HOWARD: I did. But I took them off to run.

MICHAEL: Shall we give it one more go?

PATRICK: I've not finished this.

HOWARD makes a mooing noise behind EAMON. EAMON screams. HOWARD, SHEILA and EAMON collapse in giggles.

MICHAEL: I can't believe you lot.

PATRICK: You were always frightened of the animals as a kid, Michael. And he wouldn't go to sleep if there was a moth in the bedroom with him. He was worse than Brid.

HOWARD: Bit of a cissie, were you, Michael?

PATRICK: That's just what he was. There was this one night when he went screaming into his mother because there was a little beetle climbing up the wall.

SHEILA: Awwhh.

MICHAEL: What about the time you and Liam O'Donnell held me down and made me eat a worm? You could tell them about that.

PATRICK: I never did.

MICHAEL: I remember.

PATRICK: It's terrible what boys will get up to.

SHEILA: You're telling me.

PATRICK: I'll have another go at starting this van. If I can't you could always ask that bull to tow you to Kerry.

SHEILA, EAMON and HOWARD laugh. PATRICK goes.

SHEILA: He's nice.

MICHAEL: Mmmm.

HOWARD: He's got a bit of the blarney.

MICHAEL: Fuck off Howard.

Sound of an engine turning over and resolutely refusing to start.

SCENE 4

The kitchen of the farmhouse. MICHAEL is sitting drinking coffee. EAMON enters.

EAMON: Hello.

MICHAEL: Hi.

EAMON: Someone in the bathroom?

MICHAEL: I don't know.

EAMON: Wasn't sure whether the door was stuck. Sleep well?

MICHAEL: Not really.

EAMON: Why not?

MICHAEL: This place.

EAMON: Memories?

MICHAEL: Mmm.

EAMON: You'd have been alright if you'd slept with me.

MICHAEL: You had Howard for company.

EAMON: It's not the same.

MICHAEL: Isn't it?

EAMON: No way man. I missed you. Howard could have shared with Sheila.

MICHAEL: Coffee?

EAMON: Thanks.

MICHAEL pours him some coffee.

EAMON: So when were you here last?

MICHAEL: I don't know. Fifteen years. No, it's eighteen.

EAMON: You're kidding!

MICHAEL: I came back for my mother's funeral in 1977.
There's some toast. Unless you want bacon and egg.
Patrick said there's some in the fridge.

EAMON: So have you never met your nephews?

MICHAEL: He brought them over to London once. Bout
five years ago. We all met up at the London Dungeon.

EAMON: Weird to think of you living here. Are me and
Howard sleeping in your room?

MICHAEL: No that was...

EAMON: What?

MICHAEL: Spare room.

EAMON: So which was your room?

MICHAEL: Patrick and me shared the attic.

EAMON: Will you show it me?

MICHAEL: Alright.

EAMON: Now?

MICHAEL: What about breakfast?

EAMON: We could pretend you're still living here. You're
seventeen, right? And I'm a hitchhiker and I'm staying
the night. And I get put in your bed.

MICHAEL tries to smile.

EAMON: And we lie there. Then you feel my foot on your
leg. Just a touch mind. Like you've imagined it. But you
can feel the hair on the back of your leg being touched.
And then...

He tries to put his hand down MICHAEL's trousers. MICHAEL is nervous about PATRICK walking in.

MICHAEL: If I'm seventeen you're only four.

EAMON: Mike?

MICHAEL: What?

EAMON: What's wrong?

MICHAEL: Nothing.

EAMON: You're hardly talking to me, man.

MICHAEL: I am.

He kisses EAMON.

EAMON: Let's go upstairs.

MICHAEL: I can't.

EAMON: Why not?

MICHAEL: Not now.

SHEILA enters.

SHEILA: (*Frostily.*) Morning.

MICHAEL: Morning.

EAMON: Was it you in the bathroom?

SHEILA: Yes.

EAMON goes.

MICHAEL: Sleep well?

SHEILA: Yes thanks.

MICHAEL: What time was it when you came to bed?

SHEILA: Bout two. I didn't wake you did I? You were snoring your head off.

MICHAEL: What were you doing down here?

SHEILA: Chatting to Patrick.

Pause.

MICHAEL: I couldn't get back to sleep properly.

SHEILA: Oh, I'm sorry.

MICHAEL: Kept having nightmares.

SHEILA: Oh dear.

MICHAEL: Had this horrible one where I was supposed to be looking after this baby and it kept on slipping out of my hands.

SHEILA: Oh dear.

MICHAEL: Were you hot in the night?

SHEILA: Not particularly.

MICHAEL: When I woke up I was really boiling.

SHEILA: You were probably dehydrated.

MICHAEL sighs.

SHEILA: What?

MICHAEL: I just don't like waking up hot like that.

SHEILA: Were you sweating?

MICHAEL: I don't know.

SHEILA: Well was your T shirt wet?

MICHAEL: Well...

SHEILA: Either it was or it wasn't.

MICHAEL: I was really hot.

SHEILA: If you were having night sweats you'd know it. (*Impatiently.*) For God's sake!

MICHAEL: Alright. Alright.

SHEILA: Why don't you go and talk to Eamon about your bloody symptoms?

MICHAEL: What do you mean?

EAMON enters.

EAMON: What?

SHEILA: Nothing.

EAMON: Is that your carrot moisturiser in the bathroom?

SHEILA: It's Michael's. And the under eye cream, and the eye gel.

EAMON: I used some of it.

MICHAEL: It's OK.

SHEILA: Howard up?

EAMON: Yes. He was trying to get in the bathroom when I was in there.

SHEILA: Good job he didn't do that to Michael. I got my head bitten off this morning.

MICHAEL: You kept banging on the door.

SHEILA: I wasn't sure whether there was anyone in there.

MICHAEL: Well there was.

SHEILA: He always gets constipated on holiday, Eamon. Spends hours in the toilet every morning and gets really ratty if you disturb him.

MICHAEL goes.

EAMON: Is he alright?

SHEILA: I don't know.

EAMON: He's being really funny with me, you know?

SHEILA: Is he?

EAMON: Yeah. Ever since we got to Ireland, really.

SHEILA: Well, he gets like that on holiday.

EAMON: I mean he asked me to come. He's just being so distant.

SHEILA: It'll pass.

EAMON: I don't know what I'm doing wrong, Sheila.

He starts to cry. SHEILA takes a deep breath.

SHEILA: Look, Eamon, I'm sure it's nothing. People need space sometimes. Maybe you should just back off a bit.

EAMON: But he was so keen to begin with.

SHEILA: I know. And I'm sure he still feels the same. But it's hard coming back to somewhere like this.

EAMON: Do you think it's because I'm not as intelligent as him?

SHEILA: No, of course it's not. Who said you aren't as intelligent as him anyway?

EAMON: I'm not.

SHEILA: We're all intelligent in different ways.

EAMON: He gave me this book. It takes me ages to just read one page.

SHEILA: He gets like this, Eamon. He was like it with Henry.

EAMON: What?

SHEILA: Always pushing him away. So then Henry used to go off and have affairs. Then Michael would get jealous. In the end Henry decided he was better off with someone who wanted to be with him.

EAMON: Mmmm.

HOWARD enters.

HOWARD: Morning.

SHEILA: Morning, Howard.

He looks at EAMON. SHEILA motions to him not to say anything.

HOWARD: Isn't it a lovely day? Have you seen the sky?

SHEILA: Yes.

HOWARD: Looks like it might be really hot.

SHEILA: Maybe we could go swimming in that lake we passed last night.

HOWARD: Do you think we can?

SHEILA: We should ask Patrick. We could take that illegal substance you brought, Eamon.

EAMON: Yeah.

HOWARD: What's this?

SHEILA: The fifth letter of the alphabet.

HOWARD: Eh?

SHEILA: Not A, no. And not B. Not C. Not D. But....

HOWARD: Ohhhh!

SHEILA and EAMON laugh.

EAMON: No, E!

HOWARD: I know. I've got there. How many have you brought?

EAMON: One each.

HOWARD: Right. Will Michael take one?

SHEILA: He might. He ought to!

EAMON and Sheila laugh. MICHAEL enters with more coffee.

SHEILA: You sleep well, Howard?

HOWARD: Like a log.

SHEILA: Eamon doesn't snore then?

HOWARD: He sleeps like a baby.

SHEILA: Lucky you.

MICHAEL: (*Angrily.*) You should have brought your ear plugs.

HOWARD: You don't snore do you, Michael?

SHEILA: You should hear him.

MICHAEL: You want some breakfast Howard?

HOWARD: I'm going to have an apple.

He goes and gets one from his bag.

SHEILA: What's Patrick doing?

MICHAEL: Milking. He should be in soon. He was going to try to phone the garage.

SHEILA: So what's his wife like?

MICHAEL: I went to school with her. Don't know why she married Patrick.

SHEILA: What do you mean?

MICHAEL: She was very bright – good at languages I seem to remember. Her brother went to University but girls didn't get to go in those days. She stayed at home and worked in her Dad's shop.

SHEILA: I see.

HOWARD: Anyone else want an apple?

MICHAEL: Yeah, I will actually.

SHEILA: Isn't that coffee working for you?

MICHAEL: What?

SHEILA: Doesn't that usually make you go?

HOWARD: You constipated?

MICHAEL: Not really.

SHEILA: He is.

HOWARD: There's a really good treatment for constipation.

MICHAEL: I'm going to do some eggs and bacon. Does anyone want some?

SHEILA: OK.

PATRICK enters.

PATRICK: Ahhh. Good morning.

HOWARD: You're supposed to say "Top of the morning to you."

PATRICK: Top of the morning to you.

EAMON, SHEILA and HOWARD laugh.

PATRICK: Everyone sleep well?

SHEILA: Everyone except Michael.

PATRICK: You used to be a terrible one for sleeping all the time. We could never get him out of bed.

SHEILA: Patrick, you know that lake we passed?

PATRICK: Yes.

SHEILA: Can you go swimming in it?

PATRICK: Yes you can.

MICHAEL: Have you learnt to swim, then?

PATRICK: The boys go there sometimes. You want to go?

SHEILA: We thought we might.

MICHAEL: We should try and get the van mended.

PATRICK: Well, that's what I was going to tell you. Barney wasn't there. I've got to phone back this afternoon.

HOWARD: Oh dear.

PATRICK: You can stay another night.

SHEILA: Doesn't bother me. If you don't mind Patrick.

PATRICK: I reckon I can put up with you for a bit longer. As long as you can do something about your snoring Sheila. It kept me awake half the night.

They all laugh except MICHAEL.

PATRICK: Seriously though. The place feels altogether different with someone as lovely as you in it Sheila.

EAMON makes a face and shakes his hand at SHEILA behind PATRICK's back.

HOWARD: You're making her blush, Patrick.

PATRICK: Ah now, she knows I don't mean it.

Everyone except MICHAEL laughs.

MICHAEL: You want some breakfast?

PATRICK: Dinner you mean.

MICHAEL: Lunch. Whatever.

PATRICK: That'll be grand.

MICHAEL goes.

EAMON: I'll give him a hand?

EAMON goes.

PATRICK: He looks like he slept badly.

SHEILA: He never sleeps well nowadays.

PATRICK: That's what living in London does for you.

SHEILA: Mmmm.

PATRICK: He seems tense you know?

SHEILA: Mmmm.

PATRICK: Still I think he must be feeling very sad about Henry.

SHEILA: We all are.

PATRICK: Did you know Henry well, then, Howard?

HOWARD: Pretty well.

PATRICK: I only met him the once. He seemed a nice enough fellow.

HOWARD: Are your eggs free range, Patrick?

PATRICK: Pardon?

SHEILA: Didn't you see the hens outside, Howard?

HOWARD: Oh yes! I will have one then.

He goes to the kitchen.

SHEILA: Howard was with him almost constantly while he was dying. Several times we thought it was the end and then he'd get better. But you always knew he was going to get ill again. He lost so much weight. Looked like a skeleton.

PATRICK: Terrible.

SHEILA: So unfair.

PATRICK: Well....

SHEILA: What?

PATRICK: Nothing.

SHEILA: Did Michael ever bring him here?

PATRICK: No, he wouldn't have done that.

SHEILA: Why not?

PATRICK: I think Michael was always a bit ashamed of his home.

SHEILA: Why?

PATRICK: He probably thought we'd be letting him down in front of his friends.

SHEILA: I'm sure that's not true.

PATRICK: He got a scholarship to go to Trinity College, Dublin, you know.

SHEILA: I know.

PATRICK: Mum was so proud of him. He was the light of her life. He couldn't do anything wrong at all in her eyes. It was her who was forever encouraging him to get out and go to college. Instilled it in him you might say. And he was very determined himself. Worked hard at school. Now me, I couldn't stand the school. Couldn't wait to leave.

SHEILA: Bit of a tearaway, were you?

PATRICK: Whatever gave you that idea, Sheila?

SHEILA: Can't imagine.

PATRICK: Here's me such a well-behaved, polite fella.

SHEILA: Is that what you are?

PATRICK: Did you not notice?

SHEILA: Must've slipped my attention.

PATRICK: Yes.

They laugh.

PATRICK: Anyway Michael was the clever one in the family.

SHEILA: He never talks about his Mum.

PATRICK: Things got difficult between him and Mum after Brid died.

SHEILA: What happened to Brid? Michael never really talks about it.

PATRICK: She went off the rails. Michael was all for... well... he wanted to take her to England but Mum wouldn't let her. Then she died.

SHEILA: Oh.

PATRICK: Michael blamed Mum. They had a blazing row about it. Michael left the house and never came back.

SHEILA: What did Brid die of?

PATRICK: She took some pills.

SHEILA: I see.

PATRICK: Then Mum got sick after that....We didn't know where Michael was living. By that time he'd gone over to London himself. She got the cancer, you see. Died very quickly. In the end someone gave us Henry's address. But she was already in a coma by then. She didn't know him when he came back to see her.

SHEILA: Michael's never talked about any of this.

Pause.

PATRICK: I worry about him, you know. Over in England.

SHEILA: Why?

PATRICK: I think our souls have grown apart.

SHEILA: Yes?

PATRICK: All that business with Henry while he was at the University. You know what I'm talking about.

SHEILA: You mean when he came out?

PATRICK: When he came out. That's right. That's the term for it right enough. Caused some rows so it did.

SHEILA: I'm sure.

PATRICK: It was twenty years ago Sheila. We'd hardly heard the word then.

SHEILA: What?

PATRICK: You know, homosexual, whatever you want to call it. It was like I was losing me brother. You can hardly blame Mum for not wanting to send Brid off to England with him.

SHEILA: I suppose.

PATRICK: I always used to worry that he'd be lonely as he got older.

SHEILA: He's got lots of friends.

PATRICK: Is that true?

SHEILA: Yes.

PATRICK: It was a great relief to me, you know, when I saw you and Michael together.

SHEILA: Really?

PATRICK: Yes. You hold on to him, Sheila.

SHEILA: But....

PATRICK: What?

SHEILA: It's not quite like that.

PATRICK: Is it not?

SHEILA: Michael's still gay, Patrick.

PATRICK: Oh.

SHEILA: He and Eamon are lovers.

PATRICK: But I thought....

SHEILA: What?

PATRICK: Well, Eamon and that other fella.

SHEILA: Howard?

PATRICK: Yes.

SHEILA: No.

PATRICK: Ah.

Pause.

PATRICK: So are you not married, Sheila?

SHEILA: No.

PATRICK: I can't understand why a lovely woman like you hasn't been snapped up.

SHEILA: There are other things in life, Patrick.

PATRICK: Did you never want kids?

SHEILA: Maybe.

PATRICK: I really miss my boys. They mean the world to me.

SHEILA: And your wife?

PATRICK: What?

SHEILA: Are you missing her too?

PATRICK: Oh yes. Do you not think, Sheila, that having children is the most important thing a person can do?

SHEILA: Well....

PATRICK: You're passing something on. You're helping to make the future. It's like you're giving something back to the world.

SHEILA: I suppose you could look at it like that.

PATRICK: I mean I don't judge Michael. But it's not right.

SHEILA: What?

PATRICK: His life. It's not natural, is it? And there's your man, Henry, dead.

SHEILA: So?

PATRICK: Well, he wouldn't be dead if he hadn't been what he was.

SHEILA: Patrick, I don't want to hear this.

PATRICK: What?

SHEILA: You telling me Henry deserved to die?

PATRICK: No.

SHEILA: But he brought it on himself?

PATRICK: Of course he did.

SHEILA: And Howard?

PATRICK: What?

SHEILA: (*Realising she shouldn't be telling PATRICK about HOWARD's HIV status.*) Nothing.

PATRICK: (*Shocked.*) Has he got it?

SHEILA: No.

PATRICK: What then?

SHEILA: He's tested positive. That means he could develop it.

PATRICK: My God!

SHEILA: Don't worry he brought it on himself.

PATRICK: All I mean Sheila is that sex ought to be something that happens within marriage. For procreation.

SHEILA: God! Are you telling me you never enjoyed having sex just for itself?

PATRICK doesn't know what to say. HOWARD enters.

HOWARD: I've made some tea. You want some?

SHEILA: Please.

PATRICK: No. Not for me thank you Howard.

HOWARD goes.

SHEILA: You can't get it from cups.

PATRICK: What? I know. I know.

SHEILA: Can you imagine how it must make Michael feel? Knowing that you think all that? You completely deny his whole way of life and what he is and then you moan on about how your souls have grown apart. No wonder he doesn't come back and see you.

PATRICK: Now you're getting angry with me. Don't get angry with me, Sheila.

SHEILA: I'm sorry. But you sound like a real bigot, Patrick.

PATRICK: I know how people think over in England. You've got different morals, I know.

SHEILA: You think I'm a fast woman, do you, Patrick?

PATRICK: No.

SHEILA: That's a relief.

PATRICK: But there's a reason for marriage and being faithful. I know that's not a very fashionable thing to say. Even in Ireland things are changing. Causing a lot of grief it is too. But just think, Sheila, if Michael had stayed here he might have had a family by now.

SHEILA: He might have committed suicide as well.

PATRICK: Pardon?

EAMON enters wearing an apron.

EAMON: Those boys are squabbling over how to do the eggs. Scrambled or poached?

SHEILA: Poached.

EAMON: We had to do the washing up. Doesn't look like you've washed up for months, Patrick.

PATRICK: Does it not?

EAMON: Needs a woman's touch.

PATRICK: Yes.

EAMON goes making eyes at SHEILA behind PATRICK's back.

SCENE 5

The shore of the lake. HOWARD, SHEILA and EAMON are in swimsuits. EAMON is listening to music on his walkman and dancing. HOWARD is massaging SHEILA.

SHEILA: Mmmm.

HOWARD puts some more oil on his hands.

SHEILA: It smells lovely that. What is it?

HOWARD: Clary sage.

HOWARD nudges SHEILA. They watch EAMON for a while.

SHEILA: What's he listening to?

HOWARD: Take That I think.

SHEILA: He must be exhausted.

She reaches for her camera and takes a photo of EAMON. Suddenly EAMON notices that they're watching him.

EAMON: (*Loudly.*) What?

HOWARD and SHEILA laugh at him. EAMON takes the walkman off.

EAMON: Why you laughing at me?

SHEILA: We're not.

HOWARD goes and hugs him. They laugh. EAMON sits down with them.

EAMON: (*About the view.*) Look at that.

HOWARD/SHEILA: Mmmm.

EAMON: It's so....

HOWARD: What?

EAMON: Don't know.

SHEILA: Mythic.

EAMON: Yeahhhh.

HOWARD laughs.

HOWARD: Listen to him. Yeahhhhhh.

EAMON: What?

They laugh.

SHEILA: Do you think you can get over there?

HOWARD: Patrick said they do trips round the lake.

EAMON: And what is it?

HOWARD: What?

SHEILA: A monastery.

HOWARD: Oh, the ruin.

EAMON: See Sheila knew what I meant. We must be in tune, Sheila.

SHEILA: Yeah. Imagine all those monks living over there back in the mists of time. Rowing across in their little boats.

HOWARD: Hiding from the Vikings in their round towers.

SHEILA: Howard's been reading the guide book.

EAMON: Awwhh, leave him alone.

SHEILA: I'm not being horrible, am I, Howard? You didn't think I was being horrible, did you?

HOWARD: No.

He kisses her.

HOWARD: I'm going to say this, Sheila, and I know you might think it's the drug, but I mean it. I really love you. And I just wanted to tell you. All the things you did for Henry. I think you're a wonderful person.

SHEILA: I love you too, Howard.

They hug.

EAMON: I think you're both wonderful.

They hug EAMON. They smile at each other.

SHEILA: Do you think Michael's alright?

EAMON: He was sitting hugging a tree the last time I looked.

HOWARD: Awwhhh, how sweet!

SHEILA: I wish he was here with us.

EAMON: He said he wanted to get as close to the earth as possible.

HOWARD: He should take this more often.

SHEILA: Why?

HOWARD: It would help him relax.

SHEILA: He's alright. He's lovely.

EAMON: Yeah, he is.

SHEILA: I can't understand why he doesn't want to sit and talk. That's what it makes me want to do.

EAMON: I'll go and see what he's doing.

SHEILA: Tell him to come and sit with us.

EAMON goes.

HOWARD: I think it's because, deep down, he's very lonely.

SHEILA: Maybe.

Pause.

SHEILA: That's really sad.

HOWARD: Mmmm.

SHEILA: That makes me feel so sad.

HOWARD: Yeah.

SHEILA: Why do we live our lives in London feeling so stressed and anxious when there's this?

HOWARD: Don't know. Henry always missed the countryside.

SHEILA: I know.

HOWARD: I can't wait to get to his island. Apparently it's got a sort of fort right up on the cliffs. He used to sit watching the sunset and dreaming of going to America.

SHEILA: Like St. Brendan.

HOWARD: Yes.

SHEILA: It's funny, isn't it?

HOWARD: What?

SHEILA: We spend our young lives dreaming of escaping from where we came from and the rest of the time trying to get back there.

HOWARD: You think so?

SHEILA: In some ways.

HOWARD: He used to love listening to that tape of the sea.

SHEILA: I remember.

HOWARD: Calmed him down.

SHEILA: When he was angry?

HOWARD: What?

SHEILA: He was very angry sometimes.

HOWARD: No.

SHEILA: Oh, Howard, I'm sorry. I only meant he was angry because he was dying.

HOWARD: I think he died really well.

SHEILA: Of course he did. I think it was good that he was angry. It's just that it made it hard for the rest of us sometimes.

HOWARD: I didn't find it hard.

SHEILA: No. You were wonderful to him.

HOWARD: It was what he deserved.

SHEILA: I know.

EAMON and MICHAEL enter.

SHEILA: Hello.

MICHAEL: Hi.

SHEILA: How's your tree?

MICHAEL: Very solid. Very strong.

EAMON: Like a man's thigh.

EAMON strokes MICHAEL's leg.

SHEILA: Eamon!

EAMON: What?

SHEILA: You're shocking!

HOWARD: You must have known some weird men, Eamon.

EAMON: Their bark was worse than their bite.

HOWARD groans.

SHEILA: Eh?

HOWARD: She doesn't get it.

EAMON and HOWARD laugh at her.

SHEILA: Don't laugh at me.

HOWARD: Awwhhh, Sheila, we're not.

SHEILA: Oh, I get it.

She laughs. EAMON and HOWARD laugh at her more.

MICHAEL: Any drink left?

SHEILA: Here.

EAMON: Fancy going for a swim?

MICHAEL: Haven't got my trunks.

EAMON: There's nobody about.

HOWARD: I'll come with you.

EAMON: Come on, Mike.

MICHAEL: Maybe later.

EAMON is stroking MICHAEL's leg.

SHEILA: Is it still affecting you, Eamon?

EAMON: Yeah.

SHEILA: It is me too.

MICHAEL: (*To EAMON.*) Mm, that feels nice.

MICHAEL and EAMON kiss.

SHEILA: There's Patrick.

MICHAEL: Where?

SHEILA: Coming along by the lake.

MICHAEL: Oh God!

SHEILA: What?

MICHAEL: What are we going to do?

SHEILA: Relax.

MICHAEL: He's bound to notice.

SHEILA: He won't.

EAMON and HOWARD laugh.

EAMON: I've still got one left. He could have a half.

MICHAEL: Don't be stupid.

EAMON: (*Putting his arm around him.*) It'd be nice.

MICHAEL: Don't.

SHEILA: Patrick! Over here!

EAMON: What's wrong?

MICHAEL: Just...

EAMON: What?

MICHAEL: Don't! Please

SHEILA: Maybe he's got that part. Hello, Patrick.

EAMON: Sheila wants to know about your part.

PATRICK enters.

PATRICK: You what?

SHEILA: It's lovely here.

PATRICK: You've certainly brought the good weather with you.

SHEILA: You're so lucky having all this.

HOWARD: Did you get the fuel pump?

PATRICK: No he said he'll have to order it from Dublin.

SHEILA: Oh dear.

PATRICK: I think I should give you a lift down to Kerry. Then Barney can get your van mended while we're away.

MICHAEL: What about the milking?

PATRICK: I can get Liam from the village to look after things for a couple of days.

SHEILA: Oh, thanks.

PATRICK: Not at all.

HOWARD: We could go tomorrow, then.

PATRICK: Right you are.

SHEILA: That's very kind of you, Patrick. Isn't it Michael?

MICHAEL: Mmmm.

PATRICK: That's settled then.

SHEILA: We've been sitting here imagining the monks rowing across to the monastery.

PATRICK: Is that a fact?

SHEILA: Taking secret masses.

EAMON: Secret?

SHEILA: The English wouldn't let the Catholics celebrate mass.

EAMON: Wow!

SHEILA: So people used to gather secretly at night in the open countryside and take mass in the moonlight.

EAMON: Wicked.

SHEILA: You can just see it, can't you? Gives me the shivers.

HOWARD/EAMON: Mmmm.

MICHAEL looks at PATRICK to see if he thinks they're behaving oddly.

SHEILA: It must give you a strong sense of identity to be surrounded by all this history. In England people have lost their sense of history. Over here you've still got it. It's everywhere you look.

PATRICK: But I suppose it's the reason some people feel they have to leave.

SHEILA: What?

PATRICK: All the tradition.

SHEILA: Yes.

She looks at him.

MICHAEL: She's gets over-romantic and sentimental.

SHEILA: What?

MICHAEL: Nothing.

SHEILA: Are you getting at me?

MICHAEL: No.

SHEILA: Is he getting at me?

HOWARD: No, Sheila.

He goes to put his arm round her.

SHEILA: This from the person who's just spent two hours hugging a tree.

EAMON: Don't let's argue.

PATRICK: Doing what?

Pause.

EAMON: I'd love a swim.

SHEILA: Water looks a bit dirty.

PATRICK: That's just the colour from the bog.

EAMON: I'm trying to persuade Mike to come in with me.

PATRICK: Ahhh.

EAMON: It doesn't matter if he swims in the nude, does it?

PATRICK: Well, I shouldn't think so.

EAMON: See, Mike.

MICHAEL: I don't want to.

PATRICK: You used to come here to swim.

SHEILA: He wants to get back to his tree.

HOWARD: Staring up at that muscular trunk.

HOWARD, EAMON and SHEILA giggle.

EAMON: Awwwhhh, we don't mean it, man.

He goes to touch MICHAEL. MICHAEL freezes. EAMON is hurt more than he normally would be because of the drug.

HOWARD: Come on, Eamon.

He hugs EAMON.

HOWARD: You want to come in, Patrick?

PATRICK: No.

HOWARD: Go on.

MICHAEL: He can't swim.

HOWARD: We'll look after you.

He puts his arm around PATRICK.

EAMON: Yeah.

PATRICK laughs.

PATRICK: Thanks boys, but no thanks.

He is uncomfortable with HOWARD's arm around him.

HOWARD: Get his legs, Eamon. We'll make him come in with us.

They try to pick PATRICK up.

PATRICK: No, fellas, don't.

He laughs.

HOWARD: Come on.

They are tickling him. He is laughing.

PATRICK: (*Desperately.*) No, don't please!

HOWARD: Come on.

They struggle.

PATRICK: Ahhh, don't! Please! Don't!

MICHAEL: Eamon!

In their drugged up state MICHAEL's intervention brings them up short.

MICHAEL: Leave him!

EAMON: Sorry, Patrick.

Pause.

PATRICK: I'll show you where the boys dive in.

HOWARD: Great.

EAMON, HOWARD and PATRICK leave.

SHEILA: You alright?

MICHAEL doesn't respond. He's looking at the ground.

SHEILA: Michael?

MICHAEL: Mm.

SHEILA: You alright?

MICHAEL: Mm.

SHEILA: He's really sweet.

MICHAEL: Who?

SHEILA: Eamon.

MICHAEL: Mmm.

SHEILA: You should have gone with them.

MICHAEL doesn't respond.

SHEILA: Are you feeling claustrophobic with him?

MICHAEL shrugs.

SHEILA: Patrick's so kind.

No response.

SHEILA: Isn't he?

Still no response.

SHEILA: What are you doing?

MICHAEL: Watching this beetle.

SHEILA laughs.

SHEILA: Don't you want to talk?

MICHAEL: No.

SHEILA: How can you not want to talk? It makes me want to talk.

MICHAEL: It makes me go inside.

He is still watching the beetle. SHEILA grimaces.

SHEILA: He obviously wants to communicate with you.

MICHAEL: Eamon?

SHEILA: No, Patrick. He's really trying.

Noises of HOWARD and EAMON diving into the water and gasping at the cold.

EAMON: (*Off.*) Sheila!

SHEILA: (*Calling.*) Is it nice?

HOWARD: (*Off.*) Great!

SHEILA: (*Calling.*) Doesn't it make you want to go in, Patrick?

She laughs at PATRICK's response.

SHEILA: Why did he never learn to swim?

MICHAEL: He's scared of the water.

SHEILA: Yeah?

MICHAEL: When he was small Dad threw him into Lough Derg to make him learn. He nearly drowned apparently.

SHEILA: Oh no!

MICHAEL: Mmmm.

SHEILA: Look at Howard! Eamon's trying to duck him.

They look.

MICHAEL: I'm just going back into the wood.

He leaves. SHEILA looks after him. PATRICK enters.

PATRICK: They're demented.

SHEILA: Boys will be boys.

PATRICK: Yes.

Pause.

PATRICK: Where's Michael gone?

SHEILA: For a walk.

PATRICK: Ahh.

SHEILA: I think he wants to be on his own.

PATRICK: His eyes are popping out of his head.

SHEILA: Really?

PATRICK: Yes.

She looks away so that he can't see her eyes.

PATRICK: How are you?

SHEILA: Fine. You?

PATRICK: Grand.

SHEILA: Patrick, I'm sorry.

PATRICK: What for?

SHEILA: What I said about committing suicide.

PATRICK: No. You don't have to apologise.

SHEILA: I don't know anything about what happened to Brid.

PATRICK: Maybe you're right though.

SHEILA: People commit suicide in England.

PATRICK: Mm. My wife says I'm boring – a stick in the mud.

SHEILA: Does she?

PATRICK: Yes. She suddenly got the travel bug, you know?

SHEILA: I see.

PATRICK: Started going to Italian evening class in Limerick and talking about working for the EEC. She thinks she's bloody Mary Robinson.

SHEILA: Right.

PATRICK: The thing is Sheila I've always wanted to be a farmer right from when I was small. I couldn't live in the city. She says I'm not interested in anything else. But she wasn't interested in what I was doing.

SHEILA: No?

PATRICK: I knew there was something going on, you know, but I never thought.....

SHEILA: What?

PATRICK: Well she started seeing a lot of her teacher.

SHEILA: Oh?

PATRICK: Went off to Dublin with him.

SHEILA: I see.

PATRICK: Then she thinks we can just get back together again when it all goes wrong with him. I mean that's not right, is it? She's not considering my feelings.

SHEILA: Do you want a divorce?

PATRICK: I don't believe in it.

SHEILA: What about the children?

PATRICK: They're with her. That's what I can't forgive. Putting them through all that. And I miss them so badly, you know, Sheila.

She strokes his hand. He is startled and takes his hand away.

SHEILA: I'm sorry.

PATRICK: It's OK.

SHEILA: I wasn't trying to seduce you Patrick.

PATRICK: Were you not?

SHEILA: No! God! I know you've got a pretty low opinion of women at the moment – especially English women – but really!

PATRICK: I was hoping you were.

He looks at her. They kiss. MICHAEL enters. Stands watching a moment. Then goes.

SHEILA: Howard and Eamon are coming back.

PATRICK: Yes.

They look at each other and laugh.

PATRICK: Has Michael shown you our autograph tree?

SHEILA: No.

PATRICK: We carved our names there over by the lake. I'll show you.

SHEILA: Alright. (*To HOWARD and EAMON.*) Hi!

HOWARD and EAMON enter.

SHEILA: Nice swim?

HOWARD: (*Drying himself.*) Lovely.

SHEILA: Patrick's just going to show me a tree where he and Michael carved their names.

HOWARD: Right. I'll give you that treatment, Eamon.

SHEILA: Won't be long.

HOWARD: OK.

SHEILA: Make sure Michael's alright.

HOWARD: Yeah.

SHEILA and PATRICK go. EAMON and HOWARD giggle.

EAMON: Good stuff, isn't it – E?

HOWARD: It might be the Clary sage.

EAMON: Eh?

HOWARD: (*reading from the bottle.*) "Makes you heady and euphoric. Stimulates the sexual woman in you."

EAMON laughs.

HOWARD: Lie down.

EAMON lies down. HOWARD puts some oil on his hands and starts to massage EAMON.

EAMON: Great in that water.

HOWARD: Mmmm.

EAMON: Wish Mike......

HOWARD: What?

EAMON: He's being so weird, man.

HOWARD: Forget about it.

EAMON: I don't know what he wants.

HOWARD: Neither does he.

EAMON: It just gets to me.

HOWARD: I'm sure.

EAMON: You see what he's like with me.

HOWARD: Yes.

EAMON: How did Henry feel about Michael?

HOWARD: What do you mean?

EAMON: Do you think he was still in love with him?

HOWARD: I don't know.

Pause.

EAMON: Sorry, man, that was out of order.

HOWARD: No, it wasn't.

EAMON: It was.

He touches HOWARD.

HOWARD: He's mad, Michael.

EAMON looks at him. MICHAEL enters unseen. He stands watching again. HOWARD and EAMON kiss. MICHAEL goes.

SCENE 6

High on a cliff. They are all surrounded by bags, tents, CD player etc.

SHEILA: This is a bit near the edge.

MICHAEL: Don't be daft.

SHEILA: What if it collapses?

MICHAEL: The cliff's been here for centuries.

PATRICK: What have you got in this bag, Howard?

HOWARD: Just.....

PATRICK: What?

HOWARD: My costume.

PATRICK: Your costume?

HOWARD: For the ceremony.

PATRICK: I don't understand.

SHEILA: The ashes.

PATRICK: Oh. It's a grand spot for it.

SHEILA: Fantastic view.

PATRICK: Next stop Ellis Island.

EAMON: Which way?

PATRICK points.

EAMON: Wow!

SHEILA: Don't go too near the edge.

PATRICK: Oh, I dropped my wallet, I'll just go down and get it.

He pretends to step over the cliff. EAMON and SHEILA scream.

HOWARD: When's sunset?

PATRICK: Not for a while.

HOWARD: I need time to get changed.

MICHAEL: Jesus!

HOWARD: What?

MICHAEL: Nothing.

HOWARD: We ought to get the tents up first.

PATRICK: Will I erect mine on that flat stretch further back, Sheila?

EAMON: Erect your what?

SHEILA: Good idea.

PATRICK: Do you want to help me so?

SHEILA: Aren't there still some things down by the track?

HOWARD: I'll get them.

He goes.

EAMON: Where are we going to erect ours, Mike?

MICHAEL: Right here.

EAMON: OK, then. Who's going to sleep in with us?

MICHAEL: Don't know.

EAMON: How many does your tent sleep, Patrick?

PATRICK: Two at a pinch.

EAMON: Are you going to share with us, Sheila?

SHEILA: Ummm.

EAMON: Or Howard could.

MICHAEL looks at him.

PATRICK: Right.

He picks up his tent and goes.

SHEILA: I'd better go and help him.

MICHAEL: Mmmm.

SHEILA: Unless you need a hand.

MICHAEL: We can manage.

PATRICK: (*Off.*) Will you bring the ground-sheet, Sheila?

She picks up the ground-sheet and goes.

EAMON: I think she wants to, don't you?

MICHAEL: What?

EAMON: Sleep with Patrick.

MICHAEL: I don't know. You want to assemble the poles?

EAMON: OK. Do her good.

MICHAEL: What?

EAMON: To have a little affairette with Patrick.

MICHAEL: Affairette?

EAMON: Yeah.

MICHAEL is unrolling the tent.

EAMON: You pissed off with me, Mike?

MICHAEL: No. The two bits with the spikes go at the top.

EAMON: Right. You've hardly spoken to me all day.

MICHAEL: I have.

EAMON: It was nothing, man. It was the drug.

MICHAEL: I know.

EAMON: So why are you so mad?

MICHAEL: I'm not mad. (*Angrily.*) Not like that!

EAMON: What?

MICHAEL: The smaller end fits into the bigger ends.

EAMON: Alright, alright!

MICHAEL doesn't say anything.

EAMON: Look, man, if you weren't being so fucking touchy it wouldn't of happened in the first place.

MICHAEL: Oh so now it's my fault that you and Howard got off together.

EAMON: We didn't get off together.

MICHAEL: (*Getting frustrated with the guy ropes.*) Blast!

EAMON: Mike, man.

MICHAEL: What?

EAMON: It didn't mean anything.

MICHAEL: What did you do by the way?

EAMON: Eh?

MICHAEL: Did he fuck you, did you fuck him, did you suck him off?

EAMON: Leave it, man.

MICHAEL: Don't you think I ought to know?

EAMON: What you on about?

MICHAEL: I want to know what risks you've been taking.

EAMON: I can't believe you.

MICHAEL: Did you fuck each other?

EAMON: No!

MICHAEL: But you sucked each other off?

EAMON: Mind your own business!

MICHAEL: If you're going to be promiscuous and start having unsafe sex –

EAMON: What?

MICHAEL: Oral sex is medium risk, Eamon.

EAMON: Low risk. What am I doing joining in this fucking ridiculous argument?

MICHAEL: We need to peg down the ground-sheet.

EAMON: Fuck the ground-sheet!

MICHAEL: Wouldn't surprise me if you did. You fuck everything else.

Pause.

MICHAEL: I'm sorry.

He goes to touch EAMON. EAMON won't let him.

EAMON: You're paranoid about HIV, you know that?

SHEILA enters.

EAMON: How's his erection?

SHEILA: Howard's calling. He needs some help.

EAMON: OK.

He goes. MICHAEL watches.

SHEILA: You haven't got very far.

MICHAEL: No.

SHEILA: Patrick's nearly finished already.

MICHAEL: Has he?

SHEILA: He's sent me to blow up the mattress.

MICHAEL: Mattress eh? You'll be very comfortable.

She starts blowing up the air mattress.

MICHAEL: The bag of pegs is missing.

SHEILA: It's probably down with the other bags. Michael?

MICHAEL: What?

SHEILA: Look, what happened yesterday with Patrick – it was the drug.

MICHAEL: (*About the pegs.*) Where are they?

He tries to see EAMON and HOWARD. PATRICK enters.

PATRICK: It's fun this, isn't it? Takes me right back. Our Uncle Stephen used to take us camping every summer. Remember, Michael?

MICHAEL: Yes.

PATRICK: Here, Sheila, there's an air pump you know.

SHEILA: Oh.

He hands it to her.

PATRICK: Do you want some help, Michael?

MICHAEL: I need the pegs.

PATRICK: I've got a couple left.

MICHAEL goes to look for EAMON and HOWARD.

PATRICK: You alright with that?

SHEILA: Yes thanks.

PATRICK goes off singing.

PATRICK: I'm gonna take you
On a slow boat to China......

SHEILA looks after him. She puts her head in her hands in confusion. PATRICK returns with some tent pegs.

SHEILA: (*Covering up.*) It made me dizzy.

PATRICK: Are you sure you don't want me to do it?

SHEILA: No, it's fine with the pump.

He starts pegging down the ground-sheet of MICHAEL's tent.

PATRICK: We'll be nice and cosy in that tent.

SHEILA: Look, Patrick. Maybe I should share with Eamon and Michael.

PATRICK: Oh.

SHEILA: I'm just worried about rushing things.

PATRICK: I see.

SHEILA: Don't look like that.

PATRICK: Is it something I've done?

SHEILA: No.

PATRICK: What then?

SHEILA: We hardly know each other.

PATRICK: Did you just feel sorry for me, Sheila?

SHEILA: What about Norah?

PATRICK: What about her?

SHEILA: You said she wanted to give it another try.

PATRICK: She's made her bed.

SHEILA: You couldn't forgive her?

PATRICK: You didn't ask that yesterday.

Pause.

PATRICK: Is it because of Michael?

SHEILA: What do you mean?

PATRICK: Is he jealous?

SHEILA: I don't know. That's not the point.

PATRICK: I've never met anyone like you, Sheila.

SHEILA: Don't Patrick.

PATRICK: I can't just turn it off again. Maybe that's what people do in London but I'm not like that.

SHEILA: I know. And I should have thought about that before...

PATRICK: What?

SHEILA: Before we had sex.

PATRICK: Is that what we did? I thought we were making love.

Pause.

SHEILA: This is going to take all night.

PATRICK: (*Taking the pump.*) Here. (*Pumping up the mattress.*) I thought this would be more comfortable. That was this morning when I thought we'd be lying on it together. I'm thinking I'll be lucky to even get a goodnight kiss.

SHEILA: Don't be silly.

She kisses him. EAMON enters.

EAMON: Oops.

The other two look at him.

EAMON: We've lost the bag of tent pegs.

PATRICK: I can make do with a few less.

He gives the pump back to SHEILA and goes. EAMON raises his eyebrows at SHEILA.

SHEILA: Just shut up, Eamon.

EAMON seals his lips.

SHEILA: Where's Howard?

EAMON doesn't respond.

SHEILA: Are they coming?

EAMON indicates his sealed lips.

SHEILA: Stop it.

EAMON: They started arguing about who last saw the bag of tent pegs. I left them to it. (*About the mattress.*) That's going to take a while.

SHEILA: I know.

MICHAEL enters followed by PATRICK and HOWARD.

MICHAEL: Those won't be enough.

PATRICK: Yes, they will. I've already put some in, look. And we can use stones for the guy ropes.

HOWARD: They must have got left behind in Henry's van.

MICHAEL: I put them in the land-rover myself.

HOWARD: We must have left them on the boat then.

SHEILA: Why weren't they in the bag with the tent?

MICHAEL: (*To EAMON, conciliatory.*) Will you give me a hand?

EAMON: OK.

MICHAEL starts to crawl inside the tent with the poles. The others grimace at each other. SHEILA gets her camera and takes a photo of his bottom sticking out of the tent. EAMON pinches it. PATRICK finds this hilarious.

MICHAEL: Get off.

SHEILA signals to EAMON to be careful not to annoy MICHAEL.

SHEILA: We didn't drop them on the way up here?

HOWARD shrugs.

SHEILA: Michael?

MICHAEL: What?

SHEILA: Did we drop them on the way up?

MICHAEL: How the fuck do I know?

SHEILA pokes her tongue out at him. The others try not to giggle.

MICHAEL: Now, Eamon, can you hand me that little plastic bit.

EAMON does so.

MICHAEL: No, not that.

EAMON: Alright, alright! Keep your fucking wig on!

SHEILA: Which bit is it?

HOWARD: I'll just hold on to this.

He takes one of the guy ropes.

PATRICK: Good idea.

MICHAEL: There's a little plastic saucer thing that goes under the pole to stop it making a hole in the ground-sheet.

SHEILA: Here, Eamon.

EAMON takes it and half crawls inside the tent.

MICHAEL: No! No! What are you doing?

EAMON: Nothing.

MICHAEL: Not you! Them!

HOWARD: Holding the guy rope tight.

MICHAEL: I don't want you to. I've got to lift the pole up. Mind, Eamon.

EAMON crawls out again.

MICHAEL: Let it go.

HOWARD and PATRICK let go of the guy ropes. MICHAEL lifts the pole and the whole tent collapses on him.

MICHAEL: Aowwhh.

The others get hysterical. SHEILA helps MICHAEL to get out of the tent.

MICHAEL: (*To HOWARD.*) What do you think you're doing?

HOWARD: You told us to let the guy ropes go.

MICHAEL: You're a fucking wanker, Howard.

HOWARD: You needed to keep the ropes taut.

MICHAEL: Is it your tent? Do you want to put it up? Put it up! Go on! Get in there and put it up!

SHEILA: Michael!

MICHAEL: You're the fucking expert, Howard, so put the fucking tent up!

HOWARD: I can't.

MICHAEL: So shut the fuck up. I'm fed up of listening to you telling us how to do things. You drag us all over here and make us join in some fucking ridiculous ceremony and then moan about how we're doing everything wrong. It's what you love doing, isn't it, Howard? Moaning about other people. But you never take responsibility for anything yourself.

SHEILA: Don't talk to him like that, Michael.

MICHAEL: You suddenly all pally with him, are you?

HOWARD: Piss off.

SHEILA: Leave him, Howard. There's no point arguing with him.

MICHAEL: Oh suddenly I'm being referred to in the third person.

SHEILA: Do you want to help me with this, Howard?

MICHAEL: Before you get too friendly with him you should hear some of the things he's been saying to Eamon about you, Sheila.

EAMON: Mike.

SHEILA: My leg's tired.

HOWARD starts to pump up the mattress.

MICHAEL: Apparently you took advantage of Henry when he was ill and confused and got him to change his will in my favour. It wasn't because Henry cared about me and trusted you. We tricked him into it.

EAMON: Shut up, Michael.

MICHAEL: You shouldn't tell Eamon things, Howard. He just reports it all back to me. So before you decide to be Howard's champion you ought to know all about him, Sheila. He's very two-faced.

HOWARD: (*Pumping furiously.*) Talk about the pot calling the kettle...

MICHAEL: Did you say something, Howard?

HOWARD: If anyone's two faced, it's you, Michael. Why don't you tell Sheila about the nickname you and Henry had for her?

EAMON: Look, just calm down.

MICHAEL: Get off me, Eamon.

HOWARD: What was it, Michael? You should know, you came up with it.

MICHAEL: You vicious bastard.

HOWARD: What was it? Fag hag Annie, wasn't it?

MICHAEL: Now he's playing dirty. You just can't bear the thought that Henry cared about anyone apart from you, can you, Howard?

HOWARD: I suppose you're going to say that you cared for Henry as well. You cared for him so much that you couldn't bear to be in the same room with him when he was dying. (*To the others.*) And when he did force himself to kiss Henry I found him scrubbing his lips in the bathroom afterwards.

MICHAEL: If you were such a good companion why did Henry phone me up every few months and tell me that he couldn't stand you trying to monitor his every move? Only a month before he died we had a phone-call at three in the morning. What was it he said, Sheila? If he had to spend another day with you he'd go mad?

SHEILA: Michael!

Pause.

HOWARD: Yeah, well, that's because he was a selfish bastard. Just like you. You deserved each other.

He runs away. SHEILA and EAMON look at one another.

EAMON: I'll go.

He goes.

SHEILA: (*About the mattress.*) Is this hard enough?

PATRICK: Needs a bit more.

PATRICK pumps more air into the mattress. MICHAEL crawls into the tent and puts the poles back up. SHEILA looks at PATRICK. He shrugs. MICHAEL crawls out of the tent again and starts fixing the guy ropes.

MICHAEL: What?

SHEILA: Nothing.

He continues trying to fix the guy ropes. SHEILA hands him a rock. PATRICK goes with the mattress.

MICHAEL: He makes me sick.

SHEILA: Who?

MICHAEL: Howard.

Pause.

MICHAEL: Endless whinging. Thinks he's a saint because his lover has died and he's HIV.

SHEILA doesn't respond. PATRICK returns.

MICHAEL: And Henry did say that.

SHEILA: He was ill. He was angry that he was dying.

MICHAEL: Howard threw a tantrum every time Henry wanted to do anything off his own bat. Howard wanted to keep him an invalid.

SHEILA: You still didn't have to say it to Howard like that. It was cruel.

MICHAEL: He needed to be told a few home truths.

SHEILA: Huh!

MICHAEL: What?

SHEILA: You're the one who needs to be told some home truths.

MICHAEL: Oh yeah?

SHEILA: Yes.

MICHAEL: Like what?

SHEILA: Like Howard's right. You weren't there for Henry when he needed you.

MICHAEL: (*Dismissive.*) Awhhhh.

SHEILA: You never want to face up to difficulties, Michael. He was your best friend, you'd been lovers for all those years and you weren't there for him. Not really.

MICHAEL: Not like Mother Teresa. (*Pointing to where HOWARD has gone.*) And Florence Nightingale here. (*Pointing to SHEILA.*) You both got off on it. Sitting at his bedside playing angels of mercy. Thought you were a saint, didn't you?

SHEILA: No, a fag hag.

MICHAEL: Oh, fuck off.

PATRICK: Don't talk to her like that, Michael.

MICHAEL: Oh, here comes your knight in shining armour. Feeling protective of her, are you?

PATRICK: Don't you be starting again, Michael.

MICHAEL: Has she told you yet that she only had sex with you because of what she was on? It wasn't you that made her ecstatic yesterday, Patrick, it was the drug she'd taken.

SHEILA: I'm going to find Howard.

MICHAEL: Oh, she's going to run away now. Thought I was the one who didn't face up to difficulties.

PATRICK: You don't.

MICHAEL: What's that supposed to mean?

PATRICK: You know.

MICHAEL: I don't. Perhaps you could enlighten me, brother.

PATRICK: Brid would be still alive....

MICHAEL: Don't you dare!

PATRICK: You know Brid, your sister? The one you don't talk about?

MICHAEL: You mean the one you called a prostitute? She was sixteen and pregnant and that's what her big brother called her. You want to watch out, Sheila, that's what he'll be calling you.

PATRICK: Keep your filthy mouth shut!

MICHAEL: Why? Don't you like being reminded? She wanted to have an abortion, did he tell you that? He stood by and watched our parents and the priest bully her out of it.

PATRICK: And what did you do?

MICHAEL: I arranged for her to go over to England.

PATRICK: She needed you to come home and talk to them. She wrote to you in Dublin and asked you to come home. I posted the letter for her. And you didn't come, did you? And a month later she was dead.

MICHAEL shouts and attacks PATRICK.

SHEILA: Michael!

PATRICK: Get off me.

MICHAEL: I'll fucking kill you.

PATRICK pushes MICHAEL away.

MICHAEL: I'll kill him. I'll fucking kill him.

EAMON enters.

EAMON: He climbed down the cliff. But I can't see him now. He's disappeared.

They all look at him.

SCENE 7

The same. Later. MICHAEL is sitting with two empty cans beside him. SHEILA and EAMON can be heard calling HOWARD in the distance. PATRICK enters.

PATRICK: There's no sign of him.

MICHAEL doesn't respond.

PATRICK: He wouldn't do anything stupid.

Still no response.

PATRICK: Michael!

MICHAEL: What?

PATRICK: Would he?

MICHAEL: I don't know. No. He's far too fond of himself.

Pause.

PATRICK: What time is it?

MICHAEL: Just gone eleven.

PATRICK: It'll be dark soon.

Pause.

PATRICK: Is there any more of that?

MICHAEL: This is my last.

He shakes the can and gives it to PATRICK. Pause.

PATRICK: Do you remember that time I got cut off by the sea?

MICHAEL: Cut off?

PATRICK: When we went to Connemara that time. One of the times Dad went with us. I'd been over to that island – what was it called?

MICHAEL: I don't know.

PATRICK: Omey Island! Don't you remember Omey Island?

MICHAEL: No.

PATRICK: It had a causeway that gets submerged at high tide.

MICHAEL: Oh.

PATRICK: Anyway you'd all been shouting me that the sea was coming in but I didn't hear it until it was too late. Mum and Dad wanted to get back to Clifden for supper. He was ranting and raving, "Just feckin get across here!"

MICHAEL: Sounds plausible.

PATRICK: The water was after coming up to my chest.

MICHAEL: Right.

PATRICK: And Dad wouldn't come across for me. So you came across. Do you not remember?

MICHAEL shrugs.

PATRICK: In the middle of the causeway where it was really deep you said to me, "Hold on, Patrick, I won't let you go." You were only ten yourself. And I felt so stupid having to be rescued by my little brother. Anyway when we got across Dad was getting ready to belt me one.

MICHAEL: That was nothing unusual.

PATRICK: And there was you standing in front of him saying, "Don't belt him, Daddy, he was really frightened."

MICHAEL: And did he?

PATRICK: No. Not that time.

Pause.

PATRICK: Do you not remember?

MICHAEL: Vaguely.

PATRICK: I remember because you stood up for me. It didn't happen very often that anybody stood up for me.

Pause.

MICHAEL: Do you know what I was most scared of?

PATRICK: When?

MICHAEL: With Henry.

PATRICK: Oh. What?

MICHAEL: That he was going to shit himself. Why was I so scared of that?

PATRICK: It wouldn't have been easy.

MICHAEL: I was terrified of being left on my own with him. So I used to make excuses.

PATRICK: Right.

MICHAEL: Howard was there practically twenty-four hours a day. Sheila did her bit – a few other friends – but I never stayed all night with him.

PATRICK: Look, Michael ...

MICHAEL: What?

PATRICK: What I said about Brid...

MICHAEL: I didn't come. I can't remember – I was involved with some campaign, Henry and I had just got to know each other – anyway I didn't come. Maybe if I had...

PATRICK: And maybe she'd have done it anyway.

Pause.

MICHAEL: I miss him.

PATRICK: Henry?

MICHAEL: I could have done a lot more. But I was so fucking terrified.

MICHAEL starts to cry. PATRICK is at a loss. He pats his shoulder. MICHAEL sobs. PATRICK puts his arm around him. MICHAEL collapses onto him. PATRICK holds him. As the sobbing starts to subside HOWARD enters. PATRICK suddenly sees him.

PATRICK: We wondered where you'd got to.

HOWARD: Went for a wander.

PATRICK: I'll tell the others.

He goes.

HOWARD: It was a lovely sunset.

MICHAEL: Yes.

HOWARD: The moon's rising.

MICHAEL looks up.

MICHAEL: It's full.

They look at it.

MICHAEL: He loved you Howard.

HOWARD: He took me for granted.

MICHAEL: You gave him something I couldn't.

Pause.

MICHAEL: So.

HOWARD: What?

MICHAEL: Shouldn't you be getting your costume on?

HOWARD: Oh!

MICHAEL: Isn't it time?

HOWARD: Yes. Right.

He picks up the bag.

HOWARD: (*Calling.*) Eamon! Eamon!

EAMON: (*Off.*) Howard!

HOWARD: (*Calling.*) We're going to do the ceremony.

MICHAEL: You want any help?

HOWARD: You could work the CD player.

MICHAEL: OK.

EAMON enters.

HOWARD: Over here, Eamon.

HOWARD starts to go. EAMON goes to pick up the CD player.

HOWARD: Michael's going to look after the music. Track two, Michael.

EAMON looks at MICHAEL. HOWARD goes. EAMON goes to pick up his bag. MICHAEL takes his hand. They look at each other.

MICHAEL: I might be older. Doesn't mean I'm more grown up.

SHEILA enters.

SHEILA: Is Howard alright?

MICHAEL: Yes.

EAMON: I'd better go and help.

EAMON takes his hand away and goes.

MICHAEL: We're going to do the ceremony.

SHEILA: Oh.

MICHAEL: I'm going to be DJ.

They look at each other without speaking for a moment. Then SHEILA checks her camera. MICHAEL starts setting up the music. PATRICK enters.

PATRICK: What's happening?

SHEILA: Howard's putting on his costume.

PATRICK: Ahhh.

Pause.

SHEILA: The sky's still so bright out there.

MICHAEL: I miss the long summer evenings at home.

PATRICK: At home?

MICHAEL: Yeah. At home. In London.

SHEILA: There's a star.

PATRICK: The first star of the evening.

HOWARD: OK. Put it on, Michael.

The music starts to play. HOWARD enters in a costume he has made which manages to suggest something both Druidic and camp. EAMON is his acolyte. SHEILA takes photos with the flash.

PATRICK: Jesus!

HOWARD goes to each in turn and lets them take some ashes.

PATRICK: Will I take some as well?

MICHAEL: Why not?

They proceed to the edge of the cliff.

SHEILA: (*Worried about standing too near the edge.*) Uhhhhhh.

PATRICK: You're alright.

SHEILA: Hope the wind's not going to blow it back in our faces. We could all come away with specks of Henry in our eyes.

MICHAEL: Be just like him to do that.

PATRICK: There is no wind.

The music swells. They throw the ashes. MICHAEL puts his arm around HOWARD. The ashes look like stardust. They all laugh.

THE END